I0069130

This book is a gift

From:

To:

Enjoy and Share

THIS IS
LEADERSHIP

Think You Know Leadership?

THINK AGAIN

MICHAEL KOULY

Copyright © 2020 by Michael Kouly
Design & Illustrations by Mary Shammas

All rights reserved. No part of this publication may be reproduced,
distributed, or transmitted in any form or by any means, including
photocopying, recording, or other electronic or mechanical methods,
without the prior written permission of the publisher, except in the
case of brief quotations embodied in critical reviews and certain
other noncommercial uses permitted by copyright law.

First Edition

ISBN : 978-0-9992181-9-8

This book is dedicated to YOU, dear reader, for all the leadership that you have exercised, perhaps unknowingly, and for the great potential that you embody for even more exceptional leadership.

Leadership is transformative love
in action

CONTENTS

ACKNOWLEDGMENTS

I want to acknowledge the valuable contributions of the following beautiful people: Roy Sayegh, for documenting and proofreading my thoughts clearly and efficiently. I often find it easier to think and formulate my ideas while I am pacing in our "think studio." Roy is patient and meticulous enough to adapt to my process of thinking aloud and sifting through my words to best capture what I wish to articulate, especially when the concepts are abstract and must be accurately nuanced. Mary Shammas, for adding vividness to the book by beautifully illustrating the ideas it presents. Mary also formatted the book, and designed the cover. Mary has been a creative partner in the production of all my books. Jo Lavender, for her elegant editing and instrumental recommendations. Jo's ability to transform the text into the book you see makes her an invaluable member of the team.

Many thanks are also due to the people who read the draft manuscript of this book. Their feedback and comments have been most valuable in sharpening my thoughts and clarifying them as best I can. Special thanks go to Dr. Susan Murray and Lisa Powell Graham for generously offering their thoughts and observations.

Last but not least: I want to thank YOU, dear reader, for caring about the critical subject of leadership. It is this kind of care that gives me hope that the practice of leadership will reflect the nobility and purity of this timeless form of art and science. **Thank you all.**

PREFACE

The purpose of this book is to offer an uncluttered perspective of leadership, so that we can increase our chances of exercising leadership in a more enlightened way, and helping others transform their lives and attain higher levels of endurance, abundance, fulfillment, peace and joy.

I want to highlight how crucial exercising leadership is, and to offer a reminder that whenever we have an opportunity to make an intervention and mobilize for good, we should take it. I also want to stress how important it is that we embrace the deep gratification of making a difference. Exercising leadership will give our lives profound meaning and depth, and a sense of purpose that we may not find in any other area of life. In the end, doing good is an act of love – which is what the world needs.

My hope is that this book will serve as a lighthouse, guiding us through our leadership adventures, keeping us clear of sharp rocks and dangerous currents, and allowing us to chart our courses with awareness, truth, wisdom, courage and responsibility. I would suggest that we each use our own rich experiences and trust our abilities but, if the words in this book prove useful, let them guide us and shield us from mishaps.

I have spent most of my life exploring, studying, practicing, and teaching leadership, and yet I have found that all the noise surrounding the subject is drowning out the core meaning. In this book, I hope to address the growing confusion, and resolve it by going back to the roots of the subject.

THIS IS

Leadership.

WHY THIS BOOK

Are you truly aware that you have the power to reshape reality? The power to change your life and other people's lives for the better? We all do, but it's often something we forget about in the busyness of day-to-day life, and right now, I believe it's more crucial than ever that we start remembering this power, and using it for a good purpose.

Let's look at our world and the near future we face.

There has been a lot of talk over the last few years about the fourth industrial revolution – a revolution that promises progress, prosperity, and better standards of living. Klaus Schwab, Founder and Executive Chairman of the World Economic Forum, described it this way: "We stand on the brink of a technological revolution that will fundamentally alter the way we live, work, and relate to one another. In its scale, scope, and complexity, the transformation will be unlike anything humankind has experienced before. We do not yet know just how it will unfold, but one thing is clear: the response to it must be integrated and comprehensive, involving all stakeholders of the global polity, from the public and private sectors to academia and civil society."[1] At the same time, the fourth industrial revolution poses unprecedented social, environmental, economic, and political risks.

Technology experts, like Elon Musk, Max Tegmark and many others, say the 21st century will witness major advancements in Artificial Intelligence (AI) and machine learning[2] – so much so that our reality may start looking like it belongs in a science fiction movie. Some say robots will eventually replace people's jobs[3], and computers will outstrip human intelligence.

Optimists are vocally euphoric at these prospects, which will solve many of our current problems. However, pessimists point out that the new technology will create widespread unemployment, smarter weapons, increasing the risk of catastrophic military confrontations, and will dramatically speed up the abuse of the planet's limited natural resources. The gap in the living standards between countries who are leading with AI and those less involved will dramatically increase, creating more political, security, and social tensions in a planet of ten billion people.

Whether the pessimist or the optimist is right, or the true answer lies somewhere between the two, we cannot deny that the future will vastly differ from today's world, with positives and negatives (just think how smartphones, Google, Uber, Airbnb, and social media have changed our lives in the last decade alone). We will undoubtedly face major challenges.

Consider how much the first industrial revolution required its contemporaries to change and adapt as it reshaped the world. Next, think about the second and third revolutions, which we arguably struggled to adjust to in healthy ways. We are currently facing environmental issues when it comes to plastic and the variety of its derivative products. We are still dealing with the impacts of social media, smartphones, etc. These changes have significantly affected our mental, physical, emotional, and social well-being.

All three of these revolutions were infinitesimally small in comparison to the speed, intensity, and level of adaptation that humanity will have to deal with in the coming decades. We are already starting to feel and see the impacts of the fourth revolution, with jobs being taken over by machines that operate using advanced algorithms.

Furthermore, we stand at the precipice of environmental disaster. We will either radically adapt our lifestyles, slowing down and hopefully reversing the negative effects of global warming, or we will cross a threshold that we cannot return from. Some are hopeful that advanced technology will solve many of our problems, saving us the need to alter the way we currently consume and live, but what if the speed of technological progress is not as fast as we hope it will be? Actually, we are reaching a stage where urgent global action is needed. A recent UN report projects that if we are unable to drastically change our current behaviors and slow global warming within the next decade, then the planet may experience changes that will risk the lives of all organisms on Earth, including humans.[4, 5]

Many of these challenges will fall on the shoulders of our children. They will need to find solutions to the issues that we are not resolving, cannot resolve or are creating. However, they may not be any better equipped to deal with them than we are if we don't act.

> "It is not the strongest of the species that survives, nor the most intelligent that survives. It is the one that is most adaptable to change."
>
> – *Leon C. Megginson*

With this rather grim scene set, what can we do to ensure that we are adaptable to change? We must find or cultivate leaders – but this in itself presents a huge challenge, because the term leadership has become muddled and abused, misapplied, and misunderstood. Our world is already full of touted "leaders" (politicians, CEOs, etc.) and yet we still face exponential problems. While we are making significant progress on many fronts, why are some of our global challenges becoming unnecessarily bigger? Why do we still have so much poverty when a handful of individuals have more money than dozens of countries put together? How can malnutrition and obesity continue to increase at the same time? Why is the super smart human species acting in a foolish and self-destructive way that may lead it to its extinction? Why do we keep complaining about the lack of leadership shown by the many whom we called "leaders"?

It is difficult to imagine that life could ever be entirely free of challenges like poverty, inequality, war, and other forms of suffering. The calling of leadership is not to change the nature of life, but to alleviate the unnecessary suffering that exists at all levels because of ignorance, foolishness, and hostility.

Unfortunately, leadership is becoming a cluttered, chaotic subject, immobilized by fancy lingo and complicated theories. It has been excessively commercialized, and its core meaning has faded into the background. In the past years, the lines have blurred, and we have widened the scope to include many related but not synonymous topics (e.g. power, influence, entrepreneurship, management, authority). This has further increased the confusing clutter and added to the misunderstanding of what leadership really is.

The term has not only been overused, misunderstood, and mistaught, but it has, at times, been abused and manipulated to suit specific agendas. I believe that this pattern is mainly the result of the allure surrounding this subject. Leadership is often perceived as a "sexy" subject, one that "tickles the ego," as being a "leader" tends to attract attention, importance, etc.

This book intends to **declutter** leadership, freeing it from the noise and confusion that clouds it. It will help us **rethink leadership,** and **refine the tools of leadership,** stepping away from manipulative theories. Leadership can no longer be disguised manipulation. **It cannot be art for the sake of art. We need to elevate it and give it value-based purpose and meaning.** Leadership should be about **helping others because we can**, and because **it builds a better world for everyone.** Leadership is, at its core, an act of love for those we lead.

We must bring leadership back to this core. We must reattach a moral, ethical, spiritual, and social dimension and depth to it so that people can commit to making life on Planet Earth more enduring and meaningful, and hopefully happier and more fulfilling. Leadership needs to be purpose-driven, and that purpose is clear: contribute to improving the human condition everywhere. Leadership cannot be about manipulating and influencing people with techniques, tactics, and strategies, regardless of outcome and purpose. We have tried it and it is not working, and it will definitely not work as the 21st century progresses.

In short, we cannot deal with the challenges and opportunities of the 21st century if we continue to think of leadership in much the same way as we do now, because as it has been wisely said, we cannot solve our problems with the same mindset that created them.

The only way we can succeed is if everybody bears responsibility and exercises leadership in their own contexts. It must be a collective effort, in which we all, as individuals and as groups, look at what we have the power to improve, and then put in the effort to improve it. Our world needs higher levels of consciousness and virtuous behavior more than it needs anything else right now.

To summarize, this book aims to:

1. Declutter and rethink leadership.

2. Uncover the dimensions of purpose, meaning, holistic growth, truth, and responsibility to leadership.

3. Invite everyone to tap into their intrinsic potential for greatness and exercise leadership in their own circles and beyond.

It is not a matter of choice anymore. It is time to shift the conversation, and for every individual to ask what **they** can do to help.

DISCLAIMER

The ideas put forward in this book **are not the only way** to look at leadership. There is no doubt that great minds have made, and are making, major contributions to our understanding of the leadership discipline which do not relate to this book.

The purpose of this book is to contribute to the discourse of leadership by presenting my understanding of what I have come to believe the core of leadership is, based on a lifetime of researching, teaching, and practicing this discipline.

Some concepts and words may be subject to different interpretations, especially the loaded terms that people already have their own definitions and ideas about. Some people may be tempted to argue over semantics. Sometimes subtle nuances make a big difference. This book will do its best to leave little room for interpretation, conveying my understanding of leadership in a clear-cut fashion. I know that there will be some resistance, but I ask you, dear reader, to kindly keep an open mind and consider what I have to say. If you find that you still have arguments against the concepts in this book, I highly encourage you to contribute to the discourse and sharpen the thinking on this important subject.

As my final note before we begin, in addition to some of the examples you will see in this book (some famous, others less so), I hope you will consider people you know who demonstrate leadership. Above all, I encourage you to consider how **your own actions** and how the actions of the people around you fall into the realm of leadership. I want to show you that greatness can emerge everywhere, and that acts of leadership are happening daily, quietly, and mostly behind the scenes. The people instigating these are people that you personally know, and indeed you yourself, my honorable reader.

Are you ready to explore and rediscover the true essence of leadership?

PART

1

RE-THINKING
LEADERSHIP

PUTTING LEADERSHIP IN PERSPECTIVE

Let's wind back the clock just over 70,000 years*, to the plains of the African continent. Marching in the distance is a group of *Homo sapiens,* our ancestors, making their way northeast towards Eurasia. This marks the beginning of a long journey to spread across and occupy the world. *Homo sapiens* started out, like other human species, as hunter-gatherers, foraging for food and water wherever they could find it. Moving around the African continent to begin with, they eventually ventured east towards Asia and north towards Europe. They moved from one place to another in search of food, water, and shelter. It would be tens of thousands of years before our ancestors would settle down in one place for more than a season.

What marked *Homo sapiens* out from other species? Firstly, our ability to think and overcome challenges, to craft tools, and to compare methods of doing things. This led us to spread out across the globe and learn new skills. Secondly, our ability to communicate complex ideas, which has proved indispensable to our evolution.

Fast forward a few millennia from those African plains, and we

---

* Of course, all of the information below is based on "best guess" and ties to archaeological resources, data and evidence.

might witness a group of people huddled around a campfire, telling stories or possibly cracking jokes. We are, after all, social beings, and our capacity to communicate has proved vital to our group's survival. It allowed our ancestors to create an intimate bond with members of their group, and to share information with other groups. It allowed them to hunt and gather more effectively, to shelter themselves, and to guard against predators. The ability to share knowledge and discuss experiences propelled our species into success.

Let's take another leap in time, to around 12,000 years ago. Around this point, our ancestors discovered that they were able to domesticate certain animals, and they had developed methods for better controlling their immediate environment. They settled for long periods of time, built homes, and began to grow crops; the agricultural lifestyle was born. They learned how to reap what they had sown, and how to store the grains they harvested.

Now that people across the Earth were settling and could better control their food sources, the human population exploded. Soon a group of a couple of hundred became a couple of thousand, and then villages, kingdoms, and empires began to rise.[1]

Authority

Even before we lived in large groups – but particularly once we did – we came to need an authority figure to follow. Although throughout history there have been many instances of harmful authority figures, ideally an authority figure is there to promote the well-being of their group. They should ensure members of the group collaborate and coordinate with one another. They should guide the unit towards resources and sustenance. They should help to shelter the group from unfavorable weather, and protect them from predators and other groups. They also need to keep peace within the group, dealing with conflicts before they threaten the internal harmony.

If we watch a nature documentary about any social organism, we will see that there is often a "head of the family," so to speak. In a pack of wolves, there is often a dominant male and female. In a herd of elephants, there is the head matriarch. In a community of gorillas, there is a dominant silverback gorilla. In our societies, we have appointed heads of state, city councilors, policemen and women, etc. In our businesses, we appoint executives, managers, boards of directors, and so on. In our schools, there are principals and supervisors. In our families, the parents are generally the authority.

Ronald Heifetz, of the John F. Kennedy School of Government at Harvard University, defines authority as "a contract with a person or an entity where power is entrusted for services."[2]

For the ruling body to carry out their duties, they are granted power and access to resources, so that they[3]:

1. Make decisions on behalf of the group and guide them down a path that allows the group to survive and remain sustainable – offer direction.

2. Guard the group from external threats in whichever form they come – offer protection.

3. Maintain order by:

   • Assigning different responsibilities to members of the group, and ensuring that they fulfill these responsibilities.

   • Resolving internal conflicts between different members of the group.

   • Doing what is necessary to ensure that every member of the group adheres to the established rules, rituals, regulations, and shared values.

To summarize, authority is crucial because it helps to ensure survival by securing basic resources and maintaining stability within the group. Look at almost any social structure within our world – past or present – and we will see how authority plays a role in maintaining that structure and ensuring the survival of its constituents.

However, life is not always stable and static; change is also a part of life. Although we looked to our authorities to maintain stability, we also needed to adapt whenever change came knocking on our door.

Change Is A Part Of Life

Life on Earth is dynamic, and in constant flux, from the expected cyclical changes (the seasons) to long-term shifts in the climate and landscape (e.g. the melting polar ice caps). Nature changes, but it often happens at such a slow rate that we don't realize it unless we make far-reaching comparisons between the past and the present.

For instance, I have been to cities that would have been submerged in water several hundred years ago. I have also been to places where once wide rivers have now become either dry bedrocks or thin streams. These have been slow, almost imperceptible changes that have radically altered the landscape.

Of course, there are also times when nature changes abruptly and unexpectedly, through floods, hurricanes, droughts, earthquakes, tsunamis, volcanic eruptions, etc. As you can imagine, such abrupt changes pose major threats to survival; many even have long-term consequences (e.g. the mass extinction of species millions of years ago).

Whenever changes take place, whether gradually or suddenly, life needs to adapt. Sometimes changes may give a species an advantage, and at other times, change could mean extinction if a species cannot adapt fast enough to offset its sudden shortcomings. Charles Darwin eloquently noted that only those who adapt survive; he called it "descent with modification."[4]

Changes also impact humans, and can have equally devastating consequences. The way of living, thinking, and/or behaving, as well as any established societal rules, may no longer apply to the changed environment. If that is the case, humans need to adapt, molding themselves to fit the new reality. Consider how this is evidenced throughout history; no other members of the *Homo* genus still exist, and if *Homo sapiens* had not been adaptive, we might also have gone extinct.

In our present day, the threat of survival may have less to do with physical death, and more to do with professional, psychological, and social survival. For instance, technology is now advancing at an exponential rate – so much so that we find ourselves constantly needing to learn in order to keep up. If we allow ourselves to fall short, we risk being left behind or disconnecting from the interconnected world. The good news is that it is built into our DNA to adapt and evolve when we are presented with a situation that threatens our survival and growth.

It was not stability and order that caused our ancestors to fan across the globe, seeking new lands and improved opportunities. When things must change, we look to the authority of the system to orchestrate the change.

However, when authority fails to do this, we turn our focus to acts of leadership that aim to mobilize the system and realize the change. For instance, with global warming, communities, societies and countries often turn their attention to their authority, expecting it to change laws and introduce policies that go towards dealing with issues of global warming. However, when authority fails to comply with its people's expectations, people will look to others to exercise leadership. They will rely on acts of leadership by individuals, organizations, or society to mobilize and inspire a government and its people towards the necessary change (recycling, green fuel, and other ecofriendly practices), despite the resistance that may accompany acts of adaptive and purposeful leadership.

Leadership

Many people say that humans resist change, but I disagree. As well as seeking to survive, humans seek to grow, to improve our lives, and to realize a better reality than our current one. The change associated with this growth often involves sacrifice and loss. Sometimes we must make a significant sacrifice to adapt or to grow, and this idea causes people to hesitate. It is this pain that people resist, not the change itself.

We are ready to tolerate pain if we know that our sacrifice serves a purpose. This gives us meaning, and we will gladly make changes if it will pay off in the end. As German philosopher Friedrich Nietzsche once said, "he who has a why to live can bear almost any how." However, the reward must outweigh and justify the loss.

What happens when there is no apparent justification? People are unwilling to risk their state of equilibrium and comfort for the sake of a change they don't believe is necessary. The degree of disruption that a change brings to a person's life determines how actively they will resist. Sometimes, people will fight tooth and nail to keep the things the way they are.

Never sacrifice long term benefits for short term inconveniences

Our drive to grow has, throughout our evolution, pushed us to seek new opportunities, overcome our issues, and strive towards creating an elevated reality. From this need to step out of the confines of order and harmony, and to take control of our lives and shape our realities, emerged the concept of *leadership*. However, we sometimes fail to recognize the warning signs, and may need an extra push.

People sometimes needed to be told that their reality was miserable, suboptimal, or changing and that the environment they lived in was not the same anymore. They also needed to be inspired and mobilized to break out of their shells and search for better ones. They needed to aspire towards progress and to shape their own realities, even if their lives were comfortable and stable. They needed to adapt and adopt new ways of thinking, behaving, and interpreting their reality if they wanted to survive and to grow.

Leadership is partly a description of the skills needed to mobilize people, groups, and whole societies to go through the journey of purposeful change and adaptation, which is often difficult and dangerous. Leadership's goal is to mobilize others to take responsibility, face their challenges, solve their problems, and capture the opportunities available to them for the purpose of their survival and growth.

What Does Leadership Entail?

Leadership is the process of helping a system undergo positive and meaningful adaptation so that it can ensure its survival and growth, either by:

1. Fitting into a new environment or;

2. Creating a better reality for its constituents.

In the first case, leadership is about continuing to fit into a specific environment. There will often be environmental changes that individuals have no control over. Let's say that:

1. **There have been leaps in technology and the system chooses to adopt these advances.** The system's constituents need to adapt to this change and learn as much as they can about this technology. Did they introduce this change? Most of them did not, but to live in this system and thrive, they will need to accept this change and try to fit in.

2. **A new trade agreement has been struck between two rival countries.** Most of the constituents probably did not play a part in making this trade agreement happen, but should they ignore it? No, not if they want to continue living in this system. They may need to adjust their opinions and beliefs about the new allied country and its citizens.

3. **Resources have become scarce.** If, for instance, gasoline prices skyrocket because of a shortage of imported gasoline, most of the country's residents will need to adjust their daily consumption to avoid financial troubles.

4. **Consumer preferences have radically changed.** A company cannot control what their clients want, so they need to try to adjust their products and services to accommodate major shifts.

5. **A business or professional career has collapsed because of external or personal reasons.** The business or person needs to accept their reality, accurately diagnose what went wrong, learn the lessons, and start again.

6. **Geopolitical conditions have changed around a certain country, creating substantial economic, political, and security challenges.** An individual country cannot control regional and international geopolitical developments. However, it can adapt its priorities, based on an accurate interpretation of the new reality, and it can reshape its internal policies and international relations accordingly to protect its existence and continue its development.

7. **A major illness or death has destabilized the foundation of a family.** People cannot control who gets sick or dies. However, the family members need to accept this painful reality and present a united front, so that they may find the strength to endure, and to support each other.

In all the above scenarios, people, organizations, and countries will need to adapt to these changes. They may need to adjust their way of thinking and their behavior, alter their priorities, or update their values. Adaptive changes are necessary to ensure people's continued survival within the changing system. This is where leadership steps in and helps mobilize people to adapt. The key is that leadership is constantly examining the shifting reality and considering:

- Where do the system's constituents stand?

- What is happening around them? How has the environment shifted?

- What changes must the constituents make to synchronize with the shifting environment?

When we argue with reality, reality always wins.

In the second case, leadership is about a different type of strategic adaptive change. This type of change involves mobilizing people, organizations, societies, countries, etc., to create a better reality. This is not about catching up with or reacting to contextual change, but rather deliberately instigating the change. Unfortunately, this is harder to do than in the first case. Why?

In the first case, there is a sense of urgency and instinctive threat. This, in and of itself, will motivate people to adapt. The system is changing, and its constituents see that a change is indeed necessary. Therefore, when a person exercises leadership to move these people in the direction of change, they are less likely to resist, and more likely to be convinced that change needs to happen. Apart from a few cases of adamant denial of reality, change will be seen as a necessity, not a luxury.

In the second case, people are "comfortable" with their current reality, and they are not "adequately inspired" or threatened enough to seek the opportunities at hand and enhance their lives. In other words, there is no sense of urgency.

It is difficult to persuade people to give up their "comfortable" realities and overcome the seduction of stability in order to embark on a journey of unstable transformation – even if it means potentially living a better life. People will not feel the need to "upgrade" their thinking, behavior, values, or codes of conduct for the sake of uncertain gain. Therefore, "leaders" will have a tougher time proving that adaptation is necessary. It is easier to grasp opportunities for survival than opportunities for growth.

Whether a matter of survival or of growth, adaptive leadership requires people, individually or as groups, to go through a deep introspection and gain a careful and thorough understanding of themselves. If this is neglected, they will not be able to determine:

1. What aspect(s) of their thinking, culture, mindset, etc., must be altered or removed.

2. What aspect(s) they must preserve and strengthen.

3. What new values, priorities, habits, or mindsets they must acquire.

People cannot hope to survive and thrive if they are unable to understand what is and is not working. Only by knowing oneself, others, and the system can people make the necessary changes and mobilize others to do the same.

This is necessary because the responsibility of change and transformation falls on the constituents of the system, and not on the person exercising leadership. If the majority of the system does not respond to the mobilization and change, the system's reality will remain the same, no matter how urgent change may be. The result will then be that the system's constituents will either fail to grow or, worse, fail to survive.

It is the task of the person exercising leadership to mobilize individuals so that they can make the change themselves. It is not the leader's duty to "parentally" hold people's hands through the change in a way that relieves them from their responsibility to take charge of their lives. In fact, this is a major misconception. It is the constituents of the system who will bring about a new and improved reality, with some help and a "push" or "pull" from the person exercising leadership. Survival and growth are always the direct and individual responsibility of the people involved. There is no substitute for individual and personal responsibility when dealing with reality.

It is important to note that the change leadership initiatives call for does not always entail turning people's lives upside down. The person exercising leadership should highlight the aspects of the system that will remain the same. People may be less likely to resist change if they understand that there are certain aspects of their lives that will not change. It is crucial for the person exercising leadership to be specific about what needs to change and why, as well as what aspects will continue to exist in the new reality.

Two Equally Important, Yet Different, Disciplines

Stability and predictability call for authority, while instability and abrupt change call for leadership. Authority and leadership are two different, yet equally necessary, disciplines. The context (stable or unstable) determines which discipline takes precedence. However, they both work to ensure survival and growth. Each requires different skills, tactics, strategies, characteristics, and mindsets.

Even though they are different, the same person or group can maintain stability and equilibrium (authority), and also mobilize through the uncertain terrain of meaningful adaptation to a new reality (leadership). It all depends on the circumstances and what is needed at that moment.

Although the same person can exercise leadership and assert their authority, in reality, this sometimes does not work, for several reasons. The main reason is that authority figures are expected to maintain stability; consequently, they may risk their positions if they advocate for significant change, which (as established) is sometimes unpopular.

It is also possible for a person who has exercised leadership to be granted the authority to govern the system after the "storm has passed."

The gist of it is: survival and growth is ensured when authority provides stability through direction, protection, and order, and when leadership pushes the system towards adaption and evolution.

SELF-LEADERSHIP

Leadership is not only reserved for mobilizing others: it also includes mobilizing oneself through a process of transformation. **Self-Leadership** involves acquiring the necessary skills, attitudes, and mindsets, and preparing ourselves to enhance our own lives, improve our realities, and maximize our living experiences. We can do this by altering or fine-tuning our mentalities, worldviews, beliefs, convictions, values, priorities, etc., to suit the change in the environment.

Let us assume that the working environment has changed beyond our control. This might mean a shift in:

- The working hours
- The technology used to get the job done
- The management style (perhaps a new boss)
- The priorities of the organization

Self-leadership in this context means fine-tuning or even radically changing the way we think, act, and communicate to ensure we can still function effectively in the new workplace atmosphere.

There are times where the environment remains the same, but some key opportunities for growth are available. If we know ourselves and we are aware of our strengths and shortcomings, we will know whether they are open to us or not. If they are, then we will be able to capture the opportunities.

If we cannot capture opportunities, we should assess what skills or abilities we might lack. This will allow us to look for ways to "upgrade" our repertoires of capabilities, and increase our chances of capturing the opportunities (e.g. a promotion, or a new job). This would be a case of us willingly leading ourselves to create an enhanced reality, with all the benefits that come with it – enriching the quality of our lives.

For instance, the company we work for announces its plan to open an Artificial Intelligence division in a year's time. We realize that we have all the qualifications to be a part of this division, except for expertise in the latest programming language. Therefore, we decide to take courses to learn the language and gain the necessary skills.

Self-leadership requires:

1. Purposeful self-motivation.

2. Consciously crafting our environments to remain motivated to evolve and grow.

3. Providing ourselves with whatever support structure we may need in our journeys of positive transformation.

4. Knowing ourselves on emotional, intellectual, spiritual, psychological, and physical levels so that we pay attention to all the dimensions of our being, allowing ourselves to grow holistically.

5. Honestly acknowledging our fears, insecurities, and anything else holding us back.

6. The courage to ask for help, counseling, mentoring, etc.

7. Seeking feedback to discover our blind spots.

8. The confidence to admit our weaknesses and to find intelligent ways to minimize their negative impact on our lives.

9. Removing negative people and negativity from our space, and instead surrounding ourselves with people who will inspire us, teach us, and help us be the people we want to be.

10. Burning all the dead wood that we are carrying by removing all the distractions, and the dysfunctional behaviors, habits, thoughts, and relationships that are draining us.

11. Letting go of grudges or old pains that serve no purpose.

12. Ridding ourselves of shame, guilt, and anger so that more of our energies are dedicated to building meaningful lives, rather than maintaining dysfunctional ones.

13. Adopting a learner's mindset to enhance our perception of the world and its realities so we can grow in mind, heart, and soul.

14. Taking care of ourselves and our bodies – the houses where our lives reside.

15. Gaining clarity about what matters most in life – what is necessary and should be protected, and what should be dispensed of or ignored.

16. The courage to ask ourselves difficult questions, and put ourselves in the necessary mindset to answer them (when answering these questions, you should be as specific as possible. Avoid vague answers such as "good," "better," "great," etc.):

    - What do I really want from life?
    - What do I want my psychological and physical health to be like?
    - What do I want my personal growth to be like?
    - What do I want my relationships to be like?
    - What do I want my family life to be like?
    - What do I want my professional life to be like?
    - What do I want my financial conditions to be like?

- What do I want my spiritual life to be like?

- How do I want to spend my personal leisure time?

- How do I want to contribute to society?

- What are my core strengths?

- How can I build on them?

- How can I use these strengths to offer value to the world?

- What can I do to push myself and others forward?

- If I continue as I am, where will I be in the next 5 years? 10 years? 15 years?

- If I surrender to my dysfunctional habits and foolish behavior, what will my life look like in a worst-case scenario?

- Do I want my life to end up like that?

- What impact would such an unpleasant life have on the people I love

- Would that make me fulfilled and happy? If not, where would I really want to be?

- What do I need to do differently so that I can live the life I want?

- What are my plans, if any, to have a great and fulfilling life?

- What is my plan to create progress in every aspect of my life?

Self-leadership is also essential to the success of leading others. We must lead ourselves and adopt the disciplines, habits, values, beliefs, etc., that we are attempting to lead others towards. We cannot mobilize people to go through adaptive change and ask them to alter these aspects without first being an example of the change we are advocating for. People will look at us and see what we are doing; we cannot be hypocrites if we wish to inspire. If people find discrepancies between what we are saying and what we are doing, we will probably lose our credibility.

When we apply self-mobilization and self-leadership, we will set examples that drive others. Our actions will inspire them more than our words ever could. We will need to be willing to make sacrifices and endure hardships before we can ask others to do the same. Only then can we succeed in leading others to grasp fresh opportunities for growth.

Self-leadership is often a difficult journey; it means embarking on a turbulent road, with definite setbacks and tactical failures along the way. It requires perseverance and determination, strength of character, and great focus.

It is possible that once you have considered the alternative – to remain where you are now and to keep doing what you are doing – you may decide this is not a bad choice.

It is your life, and your call.

KEY COMPONENTS OF LEADERSHIP

As established, leadership is not simple. Before we move forward, let us consider the key components that are essential for an act to be considered leadership.

Key Component No. 1: Mobilization

The word "mobilization" comes from the word "mobile": the ability to move, departing from one space and heading to another.[1] In the same sense, leadership is about getting people to move away from the dysfunctional and maladaptive aspects of their current reality, and work towards creating a better, more beneficial one.

If we separate leadership from mobilization, we will essentially be left with acts, initiatives, and interventions that don't "move" people towards a new reality. If we remove mobilization, there is no longer leadership: the entire idea of leadership will collapse. What is leadership about if it is not about mobilizing others? What would self-leadership be if it was not about mobilizing ourselves towards a better reality?

This concept is probably the most important technical aspect of leadership. However, it would be equally correct to say that it can be the most challenging, volatile, and possibly dangerous aspect of leadership. After all, we are trying to get people, or ourselves, to abandon a state of equilibrium, stability, and certainty for the chance of finding something better. We are asking others, and ourselves, to journey from a state of low stress and anxiety through an unknown, stressful terrain, which will only potentially lead to something better. However, we must overcome this and seek to mobilize ourselves and others.

Of course, mobilization does not automatically imply leadership. There are times when the intention behind an act of mobilization is malicious. History is filled with examples of people who were mobilized for selfish or detrimental reasons. Utilizing different strategies with harmful intentions is less leadership, and more negative manipulation.

We can mobilize without leadership, but we cannot lead without mobilization.

Mobilization comes in many forms. Although some people associate it predominantly with inspirational speeches and nationwide movements, mobilization can be identified even in the simplest of actions. Different types of mobilization include:

The Power of Authority. There are times when we will have some authority over the system. We might use that power to mobilize others to create and embrace significant change. For instance, many famous historical individuals mobilized their constituents from a position of authority, such as Winston Churchill, Charles De Gaulle, and Abraham Lincoln.

Motivation. We can mobilize people by motivating them, giving them a goal to work towards. Terry Fox, who suffered from cancer, decided to run across Canada to raise money for cancer research. Through his "Marathon of Hope," he was able to motivate individuals to work towards the common goal: raise money for cancer research. Despite being unable to finish his marathon (he succumbed to lung cancer), his actions motivated people all over the world to take part in an annual run named after him (The Terry Fox Run) that continues to this day.[2] The run and other initiatives by the Terry Fox Foundation have raised more than 750 million dollars for cancer research.[3]

Rational Persuasion. Mobilization can happen when we address people's minds, speaking to their intellect and providing them with reasons for change. It might only be a change in their mental state, but presenting logical arguments and swaying someone to a new mindset is mobilization.

Emotional Persuasion. People are highly receptive to initiatives that evoke their emotions. We are emotional beings, so when we appeal to people's feelings, they are more likely to embrace and instigate change. If a person succeeds in arousing anger, guilt, sadness, joy, etc., in others, s/he can mobilize them to act. For instance, it's common practice for army commanders to give evocative speeches prior to a battle. These address their soldiers' positive feelings towards their country (loyalty and patriotism), and their negative feelings towards the "evil" and threat of the enemy.

There are times when people will act irrationally because they are emotional (e.g. riots). Targeting people's hearts can be powerful. Love is one of the most powerful motivating forces, and has inspired great sacrifices and major changes throughout history. Love for oneself is crucial for self-mobilization.

Fear & Hope. People can mobilize others by striking fear into their hearts, or instilling hope. Of course, depending on the content of the message, this act of mobilization may have positive or negative consequences. Conquerors have mobilized their conquered followers by threatening their lives and those of their loved ones. Other "leaders" have used hope of a better future to revitalize individuals and mobilize them towards evolving and growing. Revolutions throughout history have operated on the hope of gaining freedom. Fear and hope have both been used to mobilize people throughout history.

Reward & Punishment. Rewards can incentivize individuals to mobilize. They will act in anticipation of a reward, whether it's material, monetary, emotional, or psychological. People will usually be more tolerant of pain and loss if they believe that their sacrifice will bring rewards. Punishment can be equally motivating, or even more so. People naturally wish to avoid pain, so it's logical that if they are threatened with punishment (material or emotional), they will be mobilized to avoid it. Rewards and punishments can both serve as strong tools to mobilize individuals towards change, whether the change is positive or negative.

Inspiration. Sometimes, all we have to do is say something or behave in a way that touches people's hearts and plucks the strings of their key values. When they are inspired, their determination to seek significant change will light an internal fire that cannot easily be extinguished.

Setting An Example. A person can mobilize others by being the example of the change they are calling for. Former Uruguayan president Jose Mujica opted not to live in the presidential residence, but in his wife's farmhouse, and he donated ninety percent of his monthly salary (which amounted to almost $10,800) to charity and small business owners.[4] Although he had a chance to live a luxurious life, he chose to set an example not only for his fellow citizens, but also for other presidents and heads of state worldwide.

Actions. Rosa Parks played a significant role in the civil rights movement by refusing to give up her seat to a white passenger. At the time, public transportation (among many other shared spaces, services, and facilities) was segregated. When the bus was filled with passengers, Rosa Parks and three other African American passengers were asked to give up their seats. Her refusal mobilized many citizens to boycott buses for more than a year.[5] Ultimately, her simple action led to a movement that ended segregation on buses and was a major step forward for the civil rights movement.

Showing Gestures Of Sacrifice. Sometimes, we can mobilize simply by choosing to make certain sacrifices. In 1948, Mahatma

Mohandas K. Gandhi went on a hunger strike, fasting for a total of six days, to protest the conflict between Hindus and Muslims in his country. His choice to sacrifice his health, and quite possibly his life, was such a moving act that it mobilized individuals to come to a peace agreement and end violent conflicts.[6]

Enduring Necessary Pain. Mobilization can happen when people find themselves in a painful situation, and they show endurance. This courage can sometimes mobilize an entire nation, or even the world. Nelson Mandela was imprisoned for 27 years before he was able to gain his freedom and the freedom of his fellow citizens.[7] Although he did not have his basic civil rights, he knew that he had to bide his time and work, enduring the hardship. His imprisonment became a matter of global importance, and his endurance helped end apartheid in South Africa.

If we fail to mobilize, we fail to lead.

Key Component No. 2: People

To exercise successful leadership, we will need to understand human behavior, group dynamics, social systems, power structures, etc. To gain the necessary understanding of the human psyche, the discipline of leadership may explore the social sciences, such as psychology, sociology, organizational behavior, political science, and anthropology.

If we do not have a clear understanding of what drives individuals or groups, we will find it difficult to mobilize people. Leadership is about helping others, and in order to do this, we need to understand the challenges they are facing.

Even when we wish to exercise self-leadership, we will need to understand what drives us and what motivates us to change.

Leadership is about mobilizing **people**. Whatever scale we are exercising leadership on, we need to remember that we are dealing with people. Our initiatives might focus on improving the environment or helping animals, but it is people who we will need to persuade. They are key to leadership initiatives.

Key Component No. 3: Purpose

Purpose is the reason that leadership is exercised. We need to be able to justify to those involved why we are doing what we are doing. Our purposes are not randomly defined; they must add value to the lives of the individuals we wish to mobilize. They must also complement the grand purpose of survival and growth for the system and its constituents. Without this key component, leadership is just technical mobilization, and possibly manipulation, which can go horribly wrong.

The purpose must satisfy one or more of these conditions:

1. To protect and save people, organizations, societies, countries, etc., from external or internal threats.

2. To deal with a problem that is draining the people's or organization's resources and may have a significant toll on the quality of their lives.

3. To capture or create an opportunity that promises significant benefits and returns these benefits to the collective. These benefits must outweigh the sacrifices that the initiative demands.

4. To intelligently and productively adapt to external and internal changes that are altering the reality of the system.

In my view, the type of leadership that we should promote and teach globally, offers hope for the future of humanity and the planet. This form of leadership is inclusive, and defined by a purpose that seeks to enhance the well-being of those around us.

Key Component No. 4: Adaptation, Evolution, and Transformation

As we mentioned earlier, adaptation and evolution are crucial for the survival of every living being on the planet, including humans. Unless we can adapt, transformation is impossible and "extinction" is inevitable – we cannot survive and thrive.

Consider how human civilizations have evolved: we have shifted away from the nomadic lifestyle and have become an interdependent, global community. This change has hinged upon our evolving intelligence, and our ability to communicate with each other and coordinate complex behaviors on a massive scale. We have adapted to environmental needs to become one of the most dominant species on Earth – one that is contemplating the possibility of expanding our civilization to other planets in the universe.

Although we share basic survival needs with all other entities, it is our ability to look for and create better opportunities that has allowed us to lead ourselves and others towards growth. We have evolved to a point where we devise ways to create progress, not simply in our own lives, but in the lives of others.

This growth also helps to further our chances of survival. If we continuously operated at critical, barely surviving levels, we would be ill-equipped to deal with a crisis when it occurred. Conversely, growth allows us to outstrip changes, giving us a margin for error, and building up our resources so we can afford setbacks.

The best strategy for survival is growth.

Leadership is about adapting to changes in the external as well as in the internal environments so that we can continue to exist. It is also about evolving our capacities to go beyond survival, and to create opportunities for growth and transformation.

PART

2

WHAT
LEADERSHIP IS

WHAT LEADERSHIP IS

Now that we have put leadership into perspective, understood how it functions, and examined its key components, it is time to look at different concepts that are part of the leadership discipline. My hope is that the information below will offer a clear foundation on which to build your own understanding of and opinions about leadership.

This section, and the one after (Leadership Is Not), are written in short, separate articles. So, feel free to peruse the articles in the order you like. You can move from one to another without following the specific order in this book. With the two following sections, you will gain a clear understanding of what I believe true leadership is, without the misconceptions that have come to be associated with it.

Leadership is a noble enterprise and discipline. It needs to be studied, understood, and practiced diligently and carefully, otherwise a person choosing to exercise leadership will risk instigating change that only brings about unnecessary chaos, loss, confusion, instability, and pain.

Let us now look at some of the things that leadership is.

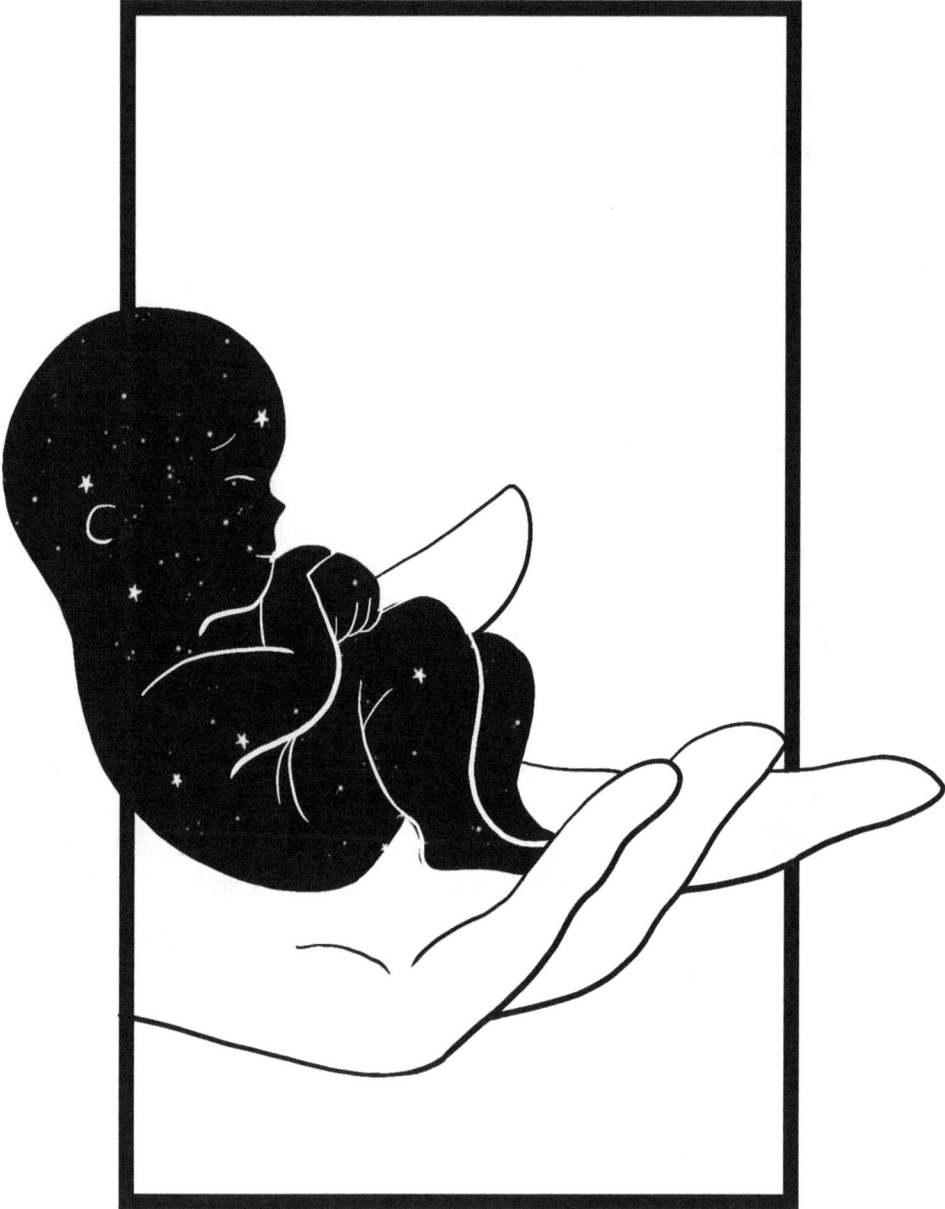

EVERYBODY IS BORN WITH THE POTENTIAL TO EXERCISE LEADERSHIP

Many of us may have heard the classical question, "Are leaders born or made?" I believe everybody can exercise leadership. I will accept the statement that "leaders are born" only on the condition that we also accept that everyone is born with a potential to lead. Leadership is not the dominion of the chosen few; instead it is a part of every person. We are born with the ability to take initiative, and to help ourselves and others survive and grow. We are all capable of caring, loving, helping, connecting, and inspiring.

Although we often assume that leadership is reserved for the few who were fortunate enough to be born with rare abilities, the truth is that most of us have exercised some form of leadership in our own lives.

If you have ever asked someone a question that made the person reconsider their thinking or behaviors in a constructive way, then you have exercised leadership, because your question has mobilized someone else to consider a better alternative. I am sure that most people have done so at some stage in their lives. As simple as this may sound, the reality is that leadership is an act, and we are all born to lead.

Some people do have, as part of their personality, the traits that are part of the repertoire of leadership capacity. This can be helpful when people wish to exercise leadership. However, this doesn't mean that others, who lack these traits, cannot learn and acquire them. For instance, some people are shy and timid, but this doesn't mean that they cannot learn to overcome their shyness and become outgoing. Think about public speaking, which many are afraid of doing. With practice,, they can overcome this fear and learn the skill.

One of the reasons that some people think leaders are born, not made, is that they view leadership as major acts of mobilization by a few who are discussed in books and media. However, I believe any person's intervention to mobilize others, even a single individual, whether at home, society, or work, to pursue a better reality for themselves is an act of leadership. Everybody, including you, has either done that or can do that.

The other reason that some people think leadership is reserved for the few is that they mistakenly equate leadership with dominance. Dominance is a common social phenomenon seen in the animal kingdom among animals who live in groups. These social animals exercise dominant power over each other, as they strive to be at the top of their social hierarchy. This phenomenon also exists in the human social systems, where people dominate others using different methods, ranging from knowledge to power of authority to brute force.

Dominance is primarily about ensuring the interests of the dominant party, largely at the expense of others. Although, the dominant entity must also care for the basic interests of its subjects so that it can continue its dominance over the long-term and avoid some sort of a revolution. Leadership, however, is primarily about promoting the interests of the group, not the sole interest of the party introducing the initiative. It is about mobilizing others for a good purpose that serves the well-being of the collective.

Different circumstances require different leadership interventions, which in turn require different skills and characteristics. Unless driven by dominance, ego, or narcissism, few people would claim to be "born" leaders. It is rarely a "life goal," or something that people aspire to for the sake of it, but instead it arises from necessity. When people see a situation which they believe could be improved, they decide to introduce leadership initiatives, and mobilize others to create a better reality. Situations, therefore, call for acts of leadership.

Abraham Lincoln was not born with special DNA that genetically predisposed him to lead. It was his tenacity, sense of fairness, and his drive that allowed him to educate himself, become a lawyer, and then become the president who introduced the Emancipation Proclamation and the Thirteenth Amendment, bringing an end to slavery in the United States.[1]

Remember, leadership is a discipline that can be learned and practiced by everyone. We need to understand human behavior and social and cultural practices, among other things. Mobilizing others to embrace beneficial change requires an in-depth understanding of the system, and this can be acquired through education, practice, and experience.

ACTION TIP:

Assertively resist the notion that leadership is exclusive to the elites, and reject any suggestions that special DNA is what allows someone to lead. Actively preach the importance of everybody taking initiative to improve the world when they can. Take every opportunity to teach yourself more about the discipline – read around the subject, engage a coach if necessary, – and get as much hands-on experience as possible. Like any learned skill, practice will help you hone your leadership capabilities.

LEADERSHIP MANTRA

We are ALL born to lead.

LEADERSHIP CREATES VALUE

The infamous Manson Family was a cult led by Charles Manson. He was charismatic, and many of his followers (approximately 100) were charmed by his personality, his claims, and his way of life. Charles Manson had the right communication and motivational skills to successfully convince many young women to follow him, becoming part of his "family." In fact, he was so effective at mobilizing others that some of his followers revered him, treating him as some kind of prophet.[2]

His followers' loyalty towards him was so immense that they eventually assisted in the murders of at least 35 people. Clearly, this cult was operating outside the confines of the law and universally accepted values, so it is safe to assume that their value system was unsound. Although he was successful in mobilizing others, Manson's flawed value system means his manipulative acts do not count as leadership by definition. Therefore, considering examples like Charles Manson and others, I pose these questions:

- Can we call such individuals successful leaders? Technically, they would be successful mobilizers and manipulators, but is that enough?

- Are these the types of "leadership" interventions that we should be promoting and teaching our children, grandchildren, and future generations about?

- Do we want such acts to be the model of leadership? Are these the types of "leaders" that create change to enhance life on this planet?

Charles Manson was without a doubt a charismatic, smart, and skillful mobilizer, influencer, and communicator, who had a clear intention and vision of what he wanted to accomplish. However, I cannot equate his manipulative acts with the acts of true leadership associated with people like Martin Luther King Jr., Susan B. Anthony, Rosa Parks, Malala Yousafzai, Greta Thunberg and others. When we take such individuals, who exercised leadership to create beneficial value for others, as our point of reference, I do not see how this former manipulator could even be grouped into the category of leadership.

Perhaps the most fundamental principle at the core of leadership is that it aims to create value. While it requires other elements, such as mobilization, it can only be considered leadership if it aims to create positive value. More specifically, an act of leadership encompasses virtues and focuses on creating an honorable and dignified reality for all the people involved.

Many individuals have sufficient people skills to nudge others to follow a certain path. However, the question is: Is this transformation an act of leadership? The answer lies in the value system that drives the transformation in the first place. If the value system is flawed (coming from a place of bad intention, exploiting the people's needs and insecurities, or operating at the expense of others), then it is an act of manipulation, not leadership.

There is more to leadership than the "technology" of mobilizing people. Consider the process of composing music. It goes beyond the technicalities of piecing different notes together. It is the intention behind the piece that evokes emotions and makes for a memorable, moving experience.

In other words, mobilizing people to change their value systems and mindsets is not considered "leadership" if it is not virtuous, and if it does not aim to promote well-being and make life better – to ensure people's survival and growth is realized. It must come from a place of good intention. It creates value by highlighting virtues and adhering to universally accepted morals.

ACTION TIP:

Always remind yourself of the purpose of your leadership act. Don't let yourself get sidetracked by unimportant or unrelated issues. When in doubt, ask whether something you are about to do will create value for others. If not, it is not leadership. Writing your purpose down can help you refer back to it and avoid any hint of confusion about where you are going.

LEADERSHIP MANTRA

How can I make the things I do and say add significant value to others?

LEADERSHIP IS MESSY

Life is not static, and people, organizations, countries, communities, etc., need to make changes accordingly. This is where a leadership intervention is needed, but sometimes the act of leadership will elicit negative reactions, which the person exercising leadership will then have to try and address or mitigate.

Let us consider the example of rocking the boat. When the waves rock the boat, things fall off the shelves. Items are displaced. Passengers feel the floor beneath them moving, and the equilibrium is destabilized. The same happens when we introduce initiatives that rock people's lives.

In response to such a shaky situation, some people may become alert, stressed, and tense. Others may become angry with those who are rocking the boat, and some might become aggressive. Others still may panic, and some of them may choose to jump off the boat to save themselves. Some might be so scared, shocked, and/or traumatized that they freeze, becoming incapable of action. All of these are reactions that a person exercising leadership must be prepared to deal with.

We must acknowledge that our actions may cause "tremors" and sometimes "earthquakes" in the system, and that these will have great impacts upon its constituents. Although the ultimate goal is beneficial, we must be prepared to deal with the reactions.

Remember that humans are highly unpredictable, and respond to stress in a multitude of different ways. We cannot know exactly what is in store for us – what reactions the change will provoke. Before undertaking an initiative, consider and plan for the emerging challenges, crises, and opponents that you will need to deal with.

This is not limited to large-scale leadership initiatives. Even a change within the home can become surprisingly messy – just as a shake-up within an organization can. Consider your own family life, and think about how specific changes might upset or agitate your family members.

I vividly recall the mess caused by transformational changes in many of the organizations I have worked for. While simple on paper, these changes and their instigators had to deal with human emotions and met extraordinary challenges during the implementation phase. I am sure you have your own personal stories that can corroborate what I have been talking about.

ACTION TIP:

Accept mess as a natural part of the process. Don't panic when things get chaotic; it is not a sign that you have made a mistake. Observe the data of the mess, and explore how things are evolving so you can better plan your future interventions (which may lead to even more productive mess).

LEADERSHIP MANTRA

I know it is going to be messy, and that's okay.

For your notes:

LEADERSHIP CAN BE A DANGEROUS ENTERPRISE

When it comes to leadership, the words "resistance" and "change" are among the first that come to mind. Leadership initiatives rarely fail because of the supporters' actions; they fail because of resistance and lack of cooperation. The resisters of an initiative will often work to undermine the initiative in any way they can. Some resisters may be more passive, not posing much of a threat, while others may be more active or aggressive in their resistance. At times, we may even encounter people who have malicious intentions towards us for the "mess" we are creating. Failure to effectively deal with and neutralize resistance can have disastrous consequences for the person exercising leadership.

The dangers of leadership can be observed on many fronts. For instance, the public domain is dotted with examples of people who lost their positions, and sometimes their lives, because they introduced significant changes that some resisted.

Let us consider examples of the more intense side of resistance. People like John F. Kennedy, Martin Luther King Jr., Mahatma Mohandas Gandhi,[3] Yitzhak Rabin, and Anwar Sadat[4] were assassinated by members of their own "tribe" or fellow citizens, because of the bold initiatives they led in their countries. Even prophets and social reformers have been threatened, betrayed, and killed for advocating radical changes in their societies.

Leadership is not something to undertake on a whim. We need to be prepared to deal with the "mess" and the risk of resistance, as well as the risk of failure, to achieve the positive change we are advocating for.

Does this mean that exercising leadership should be avoided? Not at all. Without exercising leadership there is little, if any, opportunity for people, organizations, and countries to undergo purposeful transformation that will solve problems and create opportunities. We should seize the opportunities we see to make the world better, because it's going to take the group effort of millions to overcome the challenges we are facing. However, people must be realistic and prepare for the kind of "mess" that they are creating, the risk that they are introducing, and the resistance that they may face.

ACTION TIP:

Don't play the hero, and don't take unnecessary risks. Calculated risks are acceptable, but recklessness will make everybody lose, so make sure you understand the stakes before making a choice, and choose with care.

LEADERSHIP MANTRA

I know I will be attacked. It is worth it, though.
I will be careful as I move forward.

For your notes:

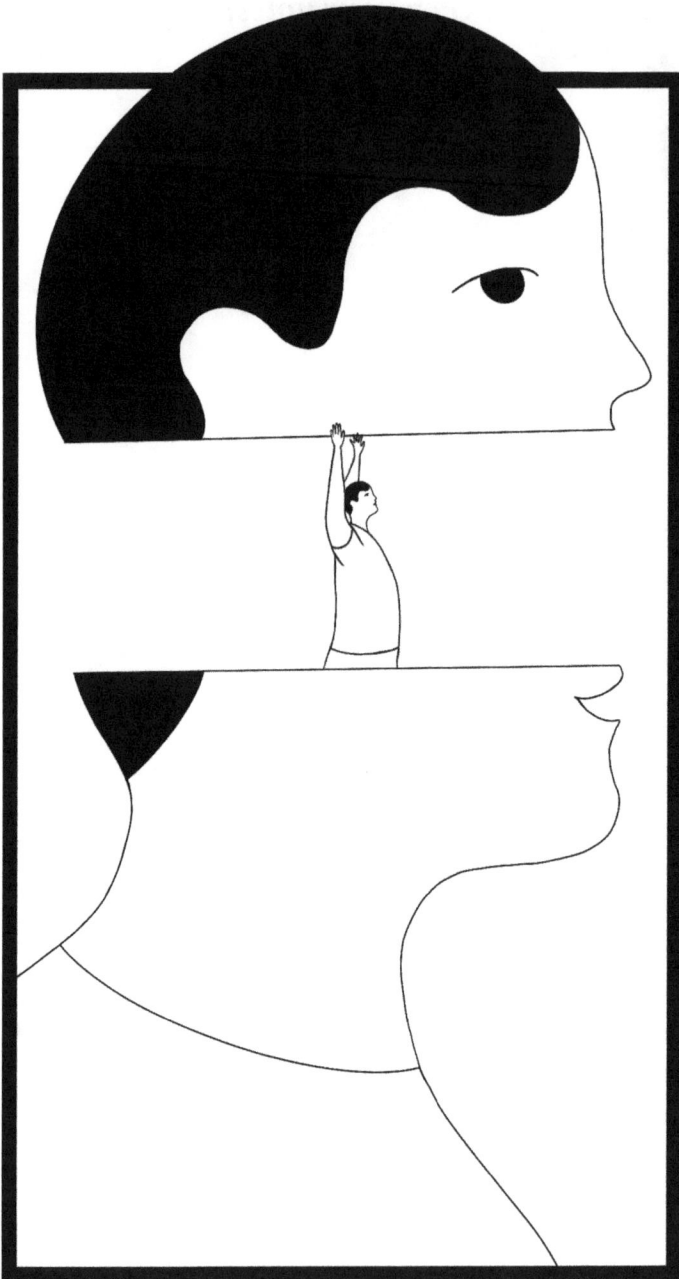

LEADERSHIP MOBILIZES TOWARDS FULFILLMENT

We have talked about leadership as the mobilization of people, organizations, and societies for the sake of creating positive and beneficial value. However, what is the purpose of mobilization, beyond just improving reality? Ultimately and ideally, the purpose is to help people achieve a sense of fulfillment, to feel that their lives have meaning, and they live life to the fullest.

How does this come to pass? Let us consider the different areas in which leadership can take place and see how fulfillment comes into the picture.

Self-Leadership

Self-leadership is about mobilizing oneself to realize one's potential and live life more abundantly. Life is meant to be engaging, not merely something to observe; we need to act in ways that help us live our lives fully, doing the things we love and care about, and pushing ourselves to persevere in even the hardest circumstances. In the end, it takes a lot of effort to realize and live our potential, becoming better versions of ourselves in the process.

Organizational Leadership

An organization achieves success when it provides fulfillment to its stakeholders.

For its **staff**, it creates an environment where they can achieve professional fulfillment. A purposeful organization imbues its staff with a sense of meaning and purpose. It breeds an environment where they can learn and grow. When the staff feel they are cared for and appreciated, they will enjoy what they are doing and find their job fulfilling. This will translate to more productivity, efficiency, innovation, and value for the organization.

An organization's **clients** are the people it aims to serve. A successful organization plays a role in its clients' fulfillment through the products and services it offers. These must satisfy a need, resolve an issue, or simply add value to and elevate its clients' lives. Adding value to the client's life is fundamental for the organization. Clients are unlikely to spend their money if what the organization is offering doesn't satisfy them in some way. When an organization's clients are properly taken care of, they will most likely end up demanding more services, which is what gives the organization continuity, and allows it to stay alive and thrive.

Ideally, a conscious, smart, adaptive, and purpose-driven organization also recognizes its ethical responsibility towards its community. It serves its **community** by ensuring the well-being of its members and enhancing their lives. It aims to elevate the system it is a part of, and it applies internal policies and regulations that aim not only to uphold its legal duty, but also to be ethical and do what is morally right by its community and stakeholders.

For instance, an organization might create jobs, internships, and volunteering opportunities, offer products and services, or invest in local projects. Such an organization understands that the stronger the community, and the greater its relationship with the organization, the more its members will contribute to the organization (as staff, clients, suppliers, or investors) and the more likely it is that the organization will thrive – it is a mutually beneficial cycle.

These organizations must also take steps to minimize any costs their presence incurs on the community; otherwise their actions will most likely backfire over the long-term. For instance, a local industrial plant that helps a community but also dumps waste into a nearby river is not focused on ensuring the community's well-being, let alone its long-term fulfillment.

Investors experience a different sort of fulfillment from the other stakeholders – financial fulfillment. Investors are mainly concerned with knowing that their investments are paying off in terms of financial returns. When the organization achieves its purpose and adds value to its other stakeholders, this will translate into a return on the shareholders' investments. In addition to this, investors may also receive emotional fulfillment if the values that govern the organization are aligned with their own values. If that is the case, they may receive emotional returns by being part of a cause they believe in, and being part of creating value through their investments.

Exercising organizational leadership is about mobilizing the organization's stakeholders, including the society in which it operates, to move closer towards their fulfillment. An intelligent organization that achieves the purpose of its existence, and adds value to its stakeholders will find long-lasting success, fulfillment, and growth.

Leadership in the Public Domain

Ideally, exercising public leadership should involve implementing laws, policies, and programs that celebrate human ingenuity, encourage growth, and emphasize the adaptive values which drive growth.

When you think about the public domain (e.g. a government and all its subsidiaries), what do you consider its purpose to be? Ideally, leadership in the public domain seeks to ensure that its constituents have the necessary conditions to achieve fulfillment in their lives. It works to supply them with the highest possible standards in the physical, psychological, social, and environmental aspects of their lives.

However, the actual transformation takes place at the personal, familial, and organizational levels. The public domain should seek to create a better reality for its people by mobilizing them to take advantage of beneficial programs, policies, etc., and creating opportunities for people to realize and pursue their true potential.

Let us consider developed countries like Sweden. Their citizens' rights and their dignity as human beings is thoroughly respected and held to the highest standards. In fact, these countries offer their citizens all the necessary services and facilities such as: healthcare, transportation, education, safety & security, access to nature, psychological support, and an abundance of other resources. Their aim is to provide a healthy environment for their citizens to live a full life.

In poorer countries – which may face daunting internal challenges (e.g. corruption) – leadership could mean mobilizing people to adopt values that will help them create a better reality. This means promoting good work ethics, professionalism, and respect for the law, the environment, and the common good.

The measure of public leadership's success is the extent to which it creates an environment that supports the individual citizens, allowing them to find fulfillment in their own lives, and in their own ways. The people must then take advantage of this environment and lead themselves and their companions towards growth and further improvement.

ACTION TIP:

Relating fulfillment to everyday life can be tricky, but make sure you bear in mind that fulfillment is the ultimate objective of everything you do. Make your leadership interventions revolve around helping people, organizations, and communities to advance towards their own fulfillment. It can help to make note of how the different elements will link up so that you have something concrete to refer to if things become chaotic. At random times, check back in with the concept of fulfillment, and make sure you feel your initiative is still on track and meaningful.

LEADERSHIP MANTRA

My purpose is to help others live a more meaningful and fulfilling life.

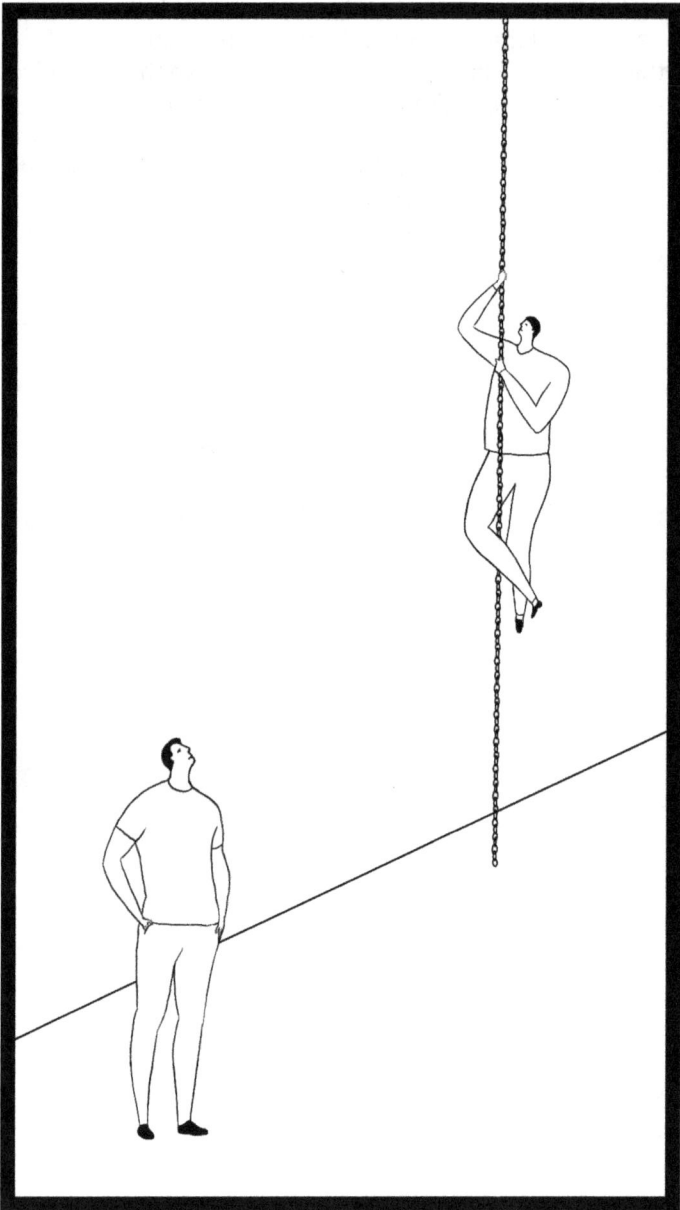

LEADERSHIP IS ABOUT DEMONSTRATING & TRYING

Leadership can happen by demonstrating, or trying to demonstrate, the behaviors that we are advocating for. We cannot make a strong case for mobilizing people to quit smoking, stop littering, or work ethically and professionally if we do not "practice what we preach." After all, "actions speak louder than words" – especially if our actions contradict what we are saying.

Remember, one form of mobilization is leading by example. A person exercising leadership demonstrates to others through their actions that change is possible. Sometimes, people will succeed, and inspire others through their example to follow suit.

Kathrine Switzer became the first woman to run as a registered contestant. In 1967, Switzer decided to run in the marathon, a race that was exclusively reserved for men at the time. Because she registered with only her initials (K.V.) and last name (Switzer), the committee mistook her for a man and assigned her a number, although her intention was not to mislead them. As she was running, the race manager attempted to literally push her out of the race because she did not qualify, in his eyes, as an official contestant. She knew that she could not quit despite the resistance because quitting the race would mean "setting women back." Therefore, she carried on and finished the race.[5]

Her actions demonstrated to men and women that gender is not a valid reason to deny women participation in athletic events; she even finished before her boyfriend, who was also a contestant in the marathon, and who helped to push the race manager off of her.[6]

However, this does not mean that we need to be perfect or successful all the time. Sometimes, leading by example means that we demonstrate persistence in the face of difficulty. When we try to find a solution, try to walk the difficult path, or try to let go of dysfunctional thinking and behavior, the "try" is itself the act of leadership. It is the inspiration, especially when we consider that we want to mobilize people to TRY to find a solution to predicaments, and to TRY to take advantage of the opportunities that are available to them.

This is particularly true when the people that we want to mobilize are skeptical, or feel powerless or helpless. By demonstrating our own attempts, we decrease the skepticism and we empower them to have faith in themselves and their capabilities, suggesting that what they see as a chasm is actually a crack. We demonstrate to them that it is acceptable to fail, provided it does not deter further efforts.

People exercising leadership are not perfect, because they might not know exactly how to traverse new territory. They might not have solutions for the new issues, circumstances, and challenges that they, and the people they are mobilizing, will face. However, this should not stop them from trying. Even trying and failing in the pursuit of a better reality is an act of leadership, and may inspire and mobilize others to try themselves.

When we try, even if we fail, we let people know that there is a better reality, and that we believe it is worth striving for. Eventually, someone will figure out how to deal with the obstacles and realize a better future, but as an act of leadership, we need to mobilize them to try.

ACTION TIP:

Take every opportunity to prove to others that you are applying the same thoughts, attitudes, and actions you are asking them to apply. You must concretely demonstrate how your thoughts are being translated into actions so that others trust you and feel encouraged to imitate you. There is no substitute for leading by example, and it is one of the best ways to mobilize others and prove your commitment to an initiative.

LEADERSHIP MANTRA

I will show them that it's worth trying, even if I don't do it perfectly.

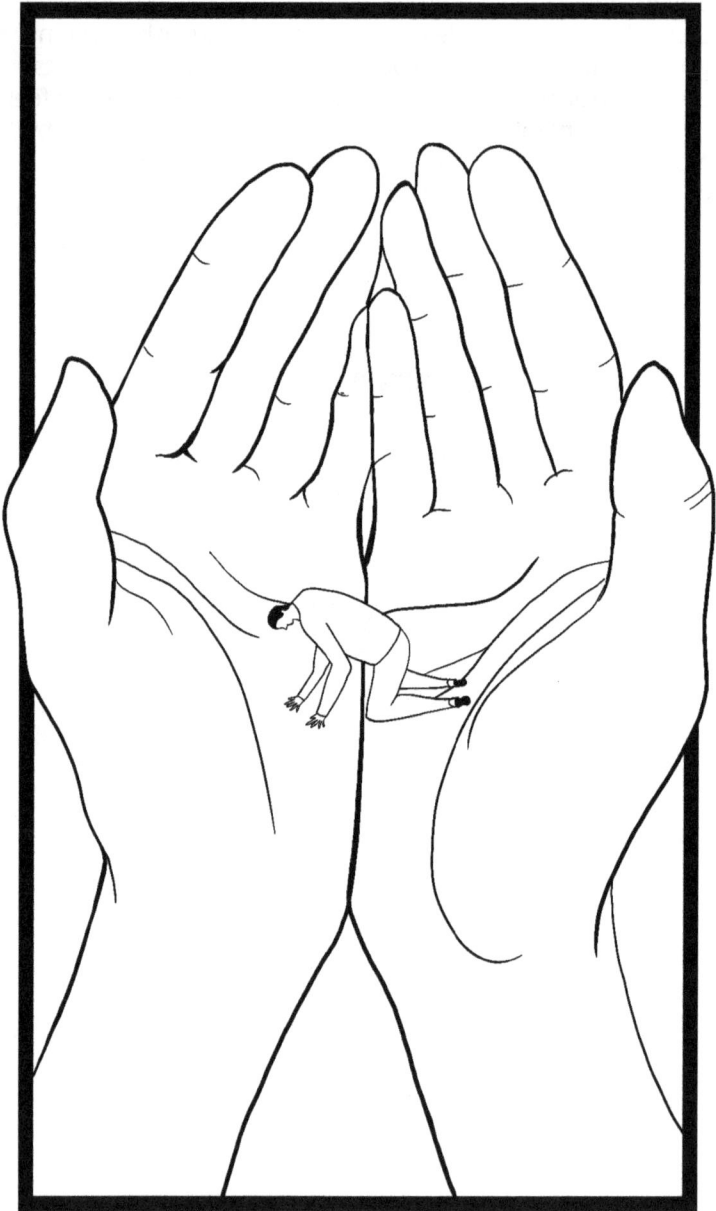

LEADERSHIP NEEDS COMPASSION

One of the drivers of leadership is compassion. Without it, we will be unable to exercise true leadership.

Compassion is what motivates us to embark on a leadership journey. Because we are compassionate, we want to reduce the suffering in the lives of those around us. Compassion also improves our ability to understand the emotions and needs of others because it includes empathy, which is necessary for us to mobilize them, and to deal with the resistance we might face.

As we express genuine compassion towards others, we must also learn to be compassionate towards ourselves. It is this compassion that allows us to take care of ourselves as we follow the uncertain, and sometimes painful, path of leadership. Once we have learned to be self-compassionate, we will be able to feel more compassion towards others, and start mobilizing them towards a better life.

Hopefully, in the end, our care will pay off. We will get gratification from knowing that we have helped people, reduced their pains, increased their resilience, and elevated their capacities. This starts with us caring about them enough to exercise leadership.

If we do not care about ourselves or others, we cannot genuinely advocate changes which will elevate reality.

An incident with the organic supermarket chain, Whole Foods, shows how compassion can translate in the business world. In 2007, in West Hartford, Connecticut, a snowstorm was brewing, and customers at Whole Foods were worried that they would not be able to purchase their products in time to reach their homes before the storm hit.

To add to their worries, the computer system on the cashier stands crashed. Then and there, the assistant manager on duty decided to let all the customers take their groceries free of charge until the system was back online.[7] This way, customers could get home without having to be held up at the store because of an error on the side of Whole Foods. The assistant manager could have easily let the customers wait, but as an act of care and concern for the customers, showed compassion on behalf of the store.

However, it is important to emphasize that compassion should not be exercised at the expense of responsibility, truth, discipline, and commitment. It should not prevent anyone from accurately interpreting reality and taking full responsibility for doing whatever will enhance survival and growth. Compassion cannot be an excuse that leads to apathy, passiveness, and avoidance of doing what is right and necessary.

ACTION TIP:

Remember that empathy can have a ripple effect, and will often spread and multiply. Create an imaginary bank account of compassion and keep making deposits. Others might be inspired to do the same. Be compassionate as often as you can, but not at the expense of your purpose to create value and do good.

LEADERSHIP MANTRA

I want to treat others with dignity, patience, and respect, especially when I lead.

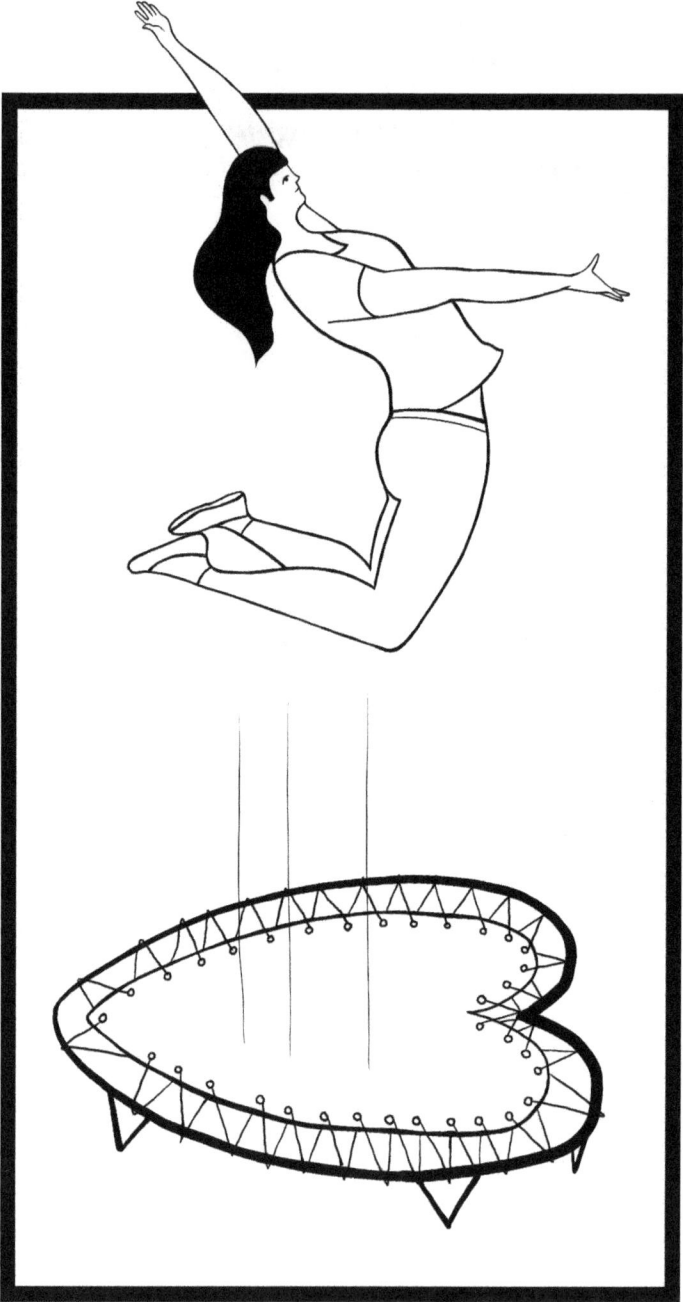

LEADERSHIP NEEDS LOVE

Another driver of leadership is love, and it is as vital to exercising leadership as compassion is.

True love is about doing whatever we can to make others happier, sometimes even at the expense of our own happiness. The essence of this love is that "your happiness is as important as mine." It is this mentality that fuels our desire to make a difference.

Love is the reason we are willing to endure hardships to elevate other people's lives. Along with compassion, love strengthens our resolve, and will help us power through despite the resistance, doubts, obstacles, negative emotions, difficulties, and everything else that makes leadership challenging and chaotic.

As with compassion, to love others, we need to experience self-love. If we love ourselves, we will constantly seek to improve our own lives as well as the lives of others, because we will understand that we deserve better, and because by loving ourselves we also teach others how to love themselves, and by lifting ourselves, we inspire others and we lift them with us. Even sacrificing for others does not mean we lack self-love.

Love gives us the energy, dedication, passion, and commitment necessary to mobilize for change and endure sacrifice, to bring about peace and create fulfillment for ourselves and others.

Love will evoke our faith in our intrinsic ability to overcome suffering, and live a life of meaning and fulfillment.

If we cannot find it in ourselves to experience love and compassion for ourselves and others, we may need to reconsider exercising leadership.

ACTION TIP:

Never lose sight of this requirement. Write down the mantra below, and put it somewhere you will see it every day. Use it as your motivator for every action. Remember it whenever you speak. Center your initiative around self-love and love for others, and it will flourish. If you ever identify actions which are not motivated by love, step back from them, examine their true motives, and redirect yourself.

LEADERSHIP MANTRA

Love is my focus and at the core of my initiative.

Mother Teresa: An Example of Love and Compassion

Mother Teresa was a nun commissioned to teach at a girls' school in India. She is said to have received a divine calling to tend to the "unloved and uncared for" in the slums of India. After petitioning the Church to allow her to abandon her convent, she received approval and established an "open-air school" to educate the "poorest of the poor," and she even set up a hospice for those who were abandoned.

She later petitioned the Church to form the congregation of "Missionaries of Charity." Eventually her congregation, with the help of donations, set up an orphanage to help abandoned children, and clinics to offer medical attention to those who could not afford regular healthcare. They even set up a leper colony to aid people suffering from leprosy.

Throughout her life, she helped numerous individuals who others avoided and ignored. She traveled to the United States, where she helped those who suffered from AIDS. She visited war zones to look after children, regardless of their faith. Her compassion and love for her fellow humans helped to inspire and mobilize others to join her congregation and aid those who were less fortunate. Her actions opened people's eyes to the reality that no matter the circumstance, we are all humans and so are deserving of love and compassion.[8]

LEADERSHIP ACCEPTS THAT NOT EVERYONE WILL BE ON BOARD

Leadership is about accepting the reality that not everyone will be in our corner. Some people will not root for our initiatives. It does not matter that the future is clear in our minds, that our understanding of the current challenges is accurate, or that the way of moving forward is obvious.

There will be people who will:

- Dispute our logic and doubt our intentions.
- Be indifferent to our interventions.
- Not be as enthusiastic as we are.
- Be actively against us and our initiatives.

We will have allies, supporters, and partners, but we will also face opponents, resisters, saboteurs, and even those who consider us enemies.

Reflection

Take a moment to recall a time in your life when you introduced a change, no matter how small.

- Did you experience some setbacks from your close friends, colleagues, family?
- Did people try to dissuade you from introducing an intervention?

Now examine the leadership journeys of those who have shaped people's lives, organizations, or countries. Consider whomever you want, and you will see that they had people who ignored them, people who supported them, and people who resisted them. You should expect the same for your initiative.

ACTION TIP:

Whenever somebody opposes you, return to this concept and use it to help yourself accept their opposition. Remember that you cannot please everyone. Even people who are extremely gentle and caring will sometimes have their actions misinterpreted, or find that their values clash with other people's values. If some people oppose your idea, say to yourself: it is not for them. Keep moving forward with the people who are on board. The others will either join later or choose their own path... and that's fine.

LEADERSHIP MANTRA

Some will go against us. Some will not care. Some will be unkind. It's okay. We all need to walk the paths which seem right to us.

For your notes:

LEADERSHIP STARTS WITH AUTHENTICITY

Leadership is about inspiration, and it cannot happen without authenticity. Many people are good at detecting when others lack authenticity. We cannot hope to keep people inspired if we start with a false foundation, proposing initiatives for the wrong reasons (e.g. personal ambition to be a "leader"). Everything we build on afterwards will be "fake," and eventually the initiative is likely to crumble – sometimes rapidly and destructively.

As Abraham Lincoln once said,

> "You can fool all the people some of the time, and some of the people all the time, but you cannot fool all the people all the time."

In the end, leadership is an authentic, wholehearted, and loving attempt to mobilize people to embark on the journey of transformation. If we wish to inspire individuals to change, we need to be authentic, honest, and upfront about our acts of leadership, and to truly believe that our interventions exist to benefit and improve the lives of others.

Strive for authenticity so that you can bring about purposeful and beneficial change.

Reflection

Take a moment to recall a time in your life where you, or someone close to you, introduced a change.

- What were the reasons for introducing your initiative? What were the reasons others had for introducing their initiatives?

- Were you, or those close to you, ever introducing change for selfish gains?

If you cannot recall an incident in your own life, think of a person or group who introduced a change.

- Who was this person or group?

- Did any of them introduce changes that were inauthentic? Were their actions coming from a "fake" place?

ACTION TIP:

Engage in initiatives and missions that you believe in. Always refer to your heart and your soul when you act. Make sure that what you are saying and doing truly reflects your beliefs, and you will have no problem being authentic to your initiative or mission.

LEADERSHIP MANTRA

I genuinely believe in what I am trying to do.
Everything I do and say is a reflection of who
I truly am.

For your notes:

LEADERSHIP IS ABOUT SPEAKING AND BRINGING TRUTH INTO BEING

While authenticity is about being real and genuine, truth is about expressing the precise intentions behind the act of leadership. Truth sees reality as it really is, leaving no room for illusions. It is about communicating the accurate nature of the current reality that needs to be changed, and the aspired reality that needs to be brought into being.

Truth is absolutely fundamental because it is the only way to create a new reality that is beneficial, meaningful, sustainable, and worth the sacrifices – a reality that will inspire and mobilize people to keep moving through challenges and keep seeking progress.

On the other hand, a reality built on lies and dishonesty is, by extension, false, and cannot be maintained – eventually everything will collapse. If truth is absent, reality will be worse off. It will be unsustainable, harmful, and people will suffer. Sooner or later things will backfire, creating distrust, disappointment, resentment, conflict, deceit, and chaos.

At its core, leadership is about speaking and bringing a better reality into existence through the power of truth.

Fruits that will improve life can only come from the tree of truth.

ACTION TIP:

Speak the truth all the time, no matter how hard it might be. Even if there is a short-term inconvenience, eventually the truth will make things better.

LEADERSHIP MANTRA

Truth will liberate us.

For your notes:

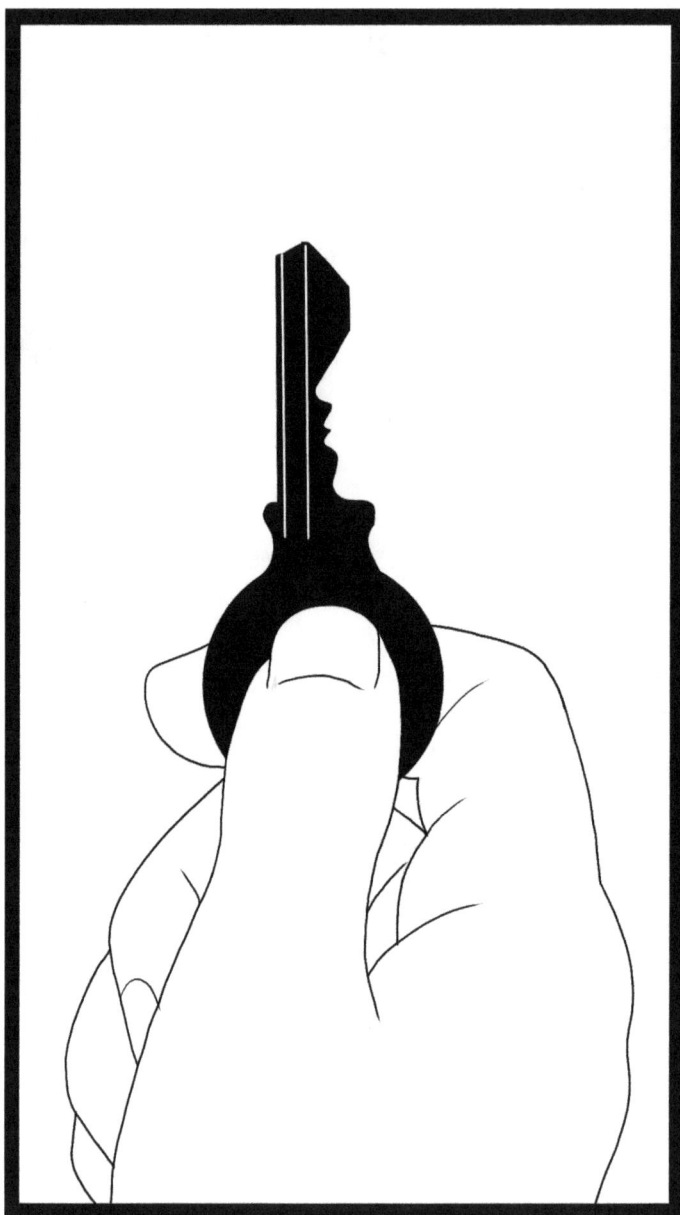

LEADERSHIP IS ABOUT EVOKING OTHERS' INDIVIDUAL AND COLLECTIVE POTENTIAL

We are all born with the potential to construct a meaningful future, despite the fact that life is often unfair. Leadership focuses on inspiring and mobilizing people to look within and unlock this potential.

Life is often painful and turbulent, and rather like an ocean. We may experience brief periods of calm, but often we are tossed by waves – sometimes even tsunamis. The good news is that we are built to withstand whatever life throws our way, because of our resilience, strength, potential, and the ability to turn challenges into either opportunities or worthwhile meaning.

Leadership is about encouraging people to tap into their potential so that they can create a better future. This potential will help them find solutions to problems that are keeping them stuck, depleting their resources, and degrading their quality of life and their well-being. Potential exists on the individual and collective level.

On the individual level, potential refers to a person's strengths, uniqueness, resilience, and capacity to learn and expand their repertoire of skills. On the collective level, potential refers to the group's strengths, resources, and capacity to cooperate and work together to realize a common fulfilling future.

Whether on an individual or collective level, exercising leadership is about helping people realize and utilize their potential so they can achieve fulfillment.

Potential can also exist externally, in the form of resources, relations, networks, knowledge, and opportunities. It is the role of leadership to help people see this external potential, the tools and possibilities that they can utilize to improve their condition, individually and collectively.

ACTION TIP:

Despair is an enemy. Encourage people to look within and around themselves for all the sources of strength and power that they can use to keep moving forward. [1]

LEADERSHIP MANTRA

There are no limits to the possibilities that people can create.

For your notes:

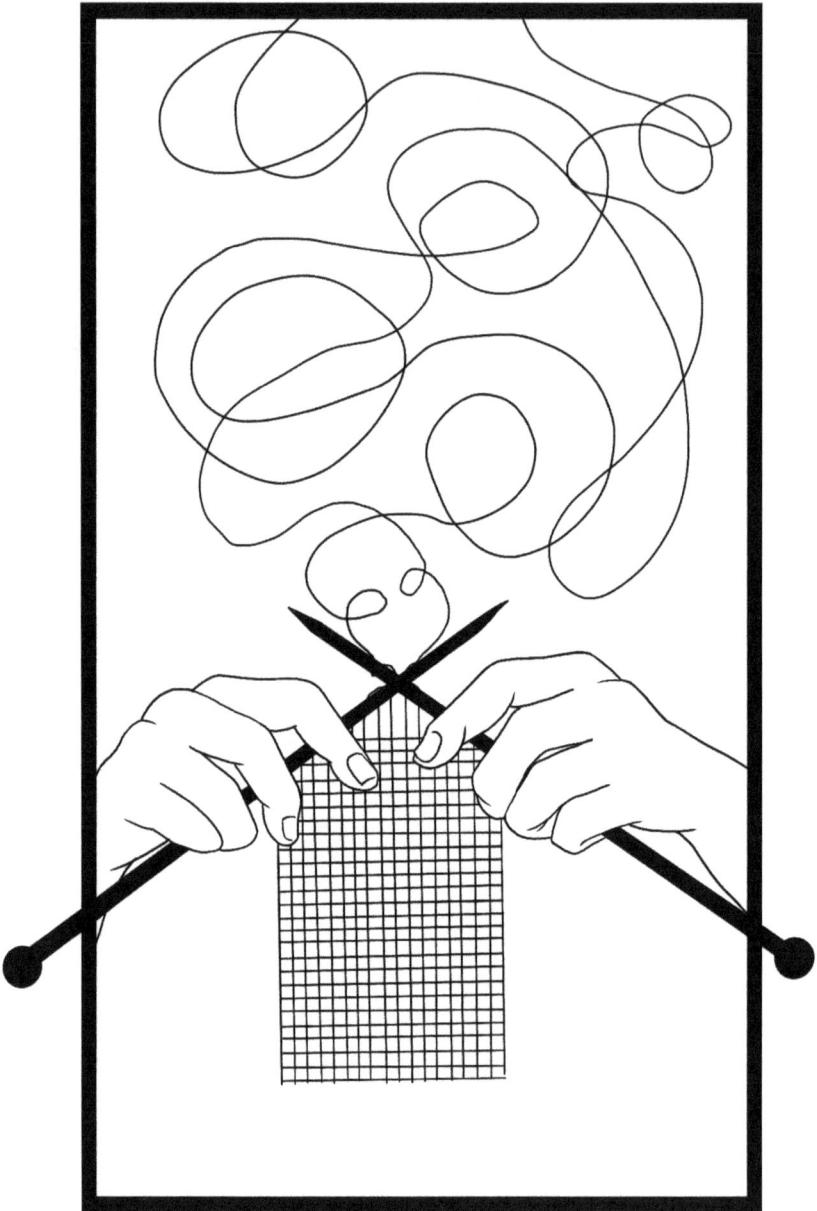

LEADERSHIP IS ABOUT TURNING CHAOS INTO ORDER

Leadership sometimes aims to turn mess, instability, confusion, and disequilibrium into order, stability, clarity, equilibrium, and more certainty, so that people, organizations, and countries can thrive. To create prosperity, we need a certain level of stability – it is a necessary condition for growth.

Let's reuse the idea of life being like an ocean. When the waves of hardship come crashing down, our lives will be plunged into instability and chaos. We may face things like business failure, death of a loved one, serious illness, betrayals, war, etc., and these things will leave us struggling with stress.

We can exercise self-leadership and deal with the mess to get our lives back on track. We can also exercise leadership and mobilize others, who have experienced similar hardships, to do the same for their lives, so that they can reinstate equilibrium and move forward towards growth. Unless we are able to find this stability, we will struggle to thrive.

ACTION TIP:

In time of distress, leadership will demand that you become a source of strength, safety, and reassurance. You will need to pull yourself and the people around you together, to endure the hardship, and emerge stronger.

LEADERSHIP MANTRA

In times of darkness, I will be the light. And in times of fear, I will be courage. And in times of despair, I will be hope. And in times of weakness, I will be strength

For your notes:

LEADERSHIP AIMS TO SERVE

Leadership is about dedication and commitment to serve others in their journey of survival and growth. Remember that a key component of leadership is purpose. At its core, purpose is about putting our unique strengths and capabilities in "service to OTHERS."

We don't ask people to uproot their comfortable lives out of spite, or just so we can be the "puppeteers" pulling their strings. We do it because we believe that our interventions will pave the way for them to live a fulfilling and dignified life.

For instance, the entire business community these days is realizing that one of the key elements of success is its ability to provide remarkable customer service and experience. In a world where most things are becoming commoditized, the notion of service is no longer a luxury. Sometimes, a company's differentiating identity is the excellence of its service.

Take, for example, Elon Musk, the CEO of Tesla. In June of 2014, Musk decided to release all of Tesla's patents so others might use Tesla's technology to improve upon and create alternative and sustainable forms of transport. His dedication to serve not only his customers but the planet overrode his desire to create a niche market. Instead, he chose to encourage others to follow in Tesla's footsteps, in the hopes that electric cars would become the norm on our roads – so that they might become more readily available and mainstream. His dedication is reflected in this excerpt from an article he wrote back in 2014, "We believe that Tesla, other companies making electric cars, and the world would all benefit from a common, rapidly-evolving technology platform."[9]

Let us consider a non-corporate example of service. Dorothea Dix was a teacher, governess, author, abolitionist, and social reformer. Her drive to serve her fellow human beings led to her spearheading social reforms to help the mentally ill, who at the time often did not have proper institutions to receive treatment. By investigating the conditions and writing reports on them, she succeeded in convincing legislators to build or modernize public mental institutions in 14 states.

In addition, witnessing the cruelty with which many mentally ill prisoners were treated drove her to call for separating them from the general prison population, and to advocate for gentler treatment. She also traveled to Europe, investigated the conditions there, and was able to convince the Pope at the time (Pope Pius IX) to support her efforts.

Later in her life, she was able to inspire better medical treatment for wounded soldiers during the American Civil War.[10] She experienced bouts of depression and illness throughout her life, but her compassion and love for her fellow humans drove her to introduce change in the system, inspiring others locally and internationally throughout her lifetime and in the future. Her work improved the quality of life for thousands of people.

"Whoever wants to become great among you must be your servant, and whoever wants to be first must be slave of all."

– Mark 10:43

ACTION TIP:

Think about how you are serving others, and not just within the context of the initiative. Helping others improves your ability to connect with and understand people, which will help you implement effective, beneficial initiatives. Make a habit out of logging all the ways in which you help the people around you, and be proud of yourself for this. Align yourself with service wherever possible.

LEADERSHIP MANTRA

I will continue to serve my people and the initiative.

Helping others improves the world, whether it's related to an initiative or not. I will always choose respect, empathy, and care.

LEADERSHIP DEMANDS RESILIENCE

Resilience is a necessary trait if we want to exercise leadership. This is not surprising when we consider the possible obstacles that we will encounter, ranging from chance inconveniences to intense, active resistance. Remember that many initiatives fail initially. Being able to get back up and carry on can make the difference, and will require us to exercise resilience.

In addition to this, resilience will allow us and our people to remain hopeful. Hope will help us see past hardships and discomforts, and work towards a better future; without it, we may succumb to pressures and give up.

Furthermore, our resilience will in itself mobilize others to push through difficulties too. When they see that we are not giving up, this may strengthen their resolve, and inspire them to keep progressing. It will prove our dedication to the changes we are proposing, and will ensure others believe we are genuine.

In the end, resilience is a necessary companion to exercising leadership, because the process can be difficult, dangerous, and immensely stressful.

Reflection

We all have at least one person (someone we either know or have heard of) who we admire for their perseverance and resilience. Take a moment to think of this person(s).

- What have they gone through in their lives?
- How did they demonstrate resilience in the face of difficulty?
- Did they exercise leadership? How so?
- What can you learn from them?

Now, considering the ups and downs of your own life, how have you shown resilience?

"Anyone can hold the helm when the sea is calm."

– Publilius Syrus

ACTION TIP:

As well as the suggestions above, consider choosing someone whose endurance you admire, and use them as your inspiration to keep going. Motivate yourself with successes and realistic goals to keep yourself moving.

LEADERSHIP MANTRA

There is no going back. When I fall, I will stand up again and continue. Setbacks won't deter me from seeing my initiative through.

For your notes:

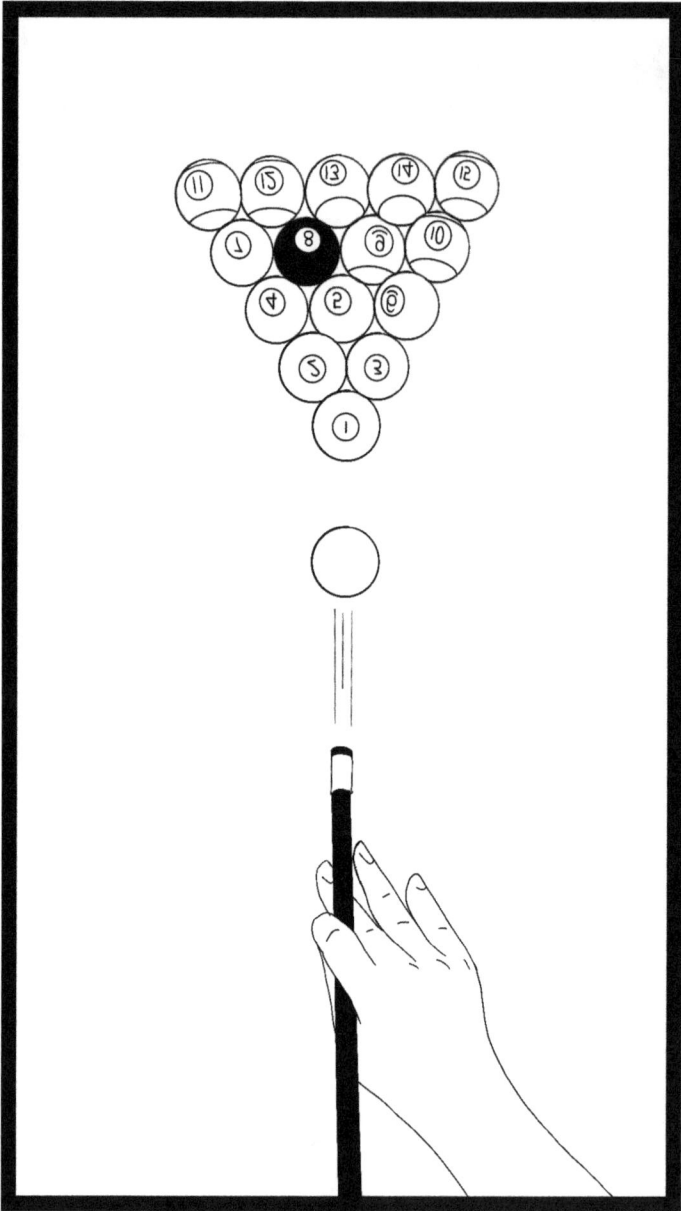

LEADERSHIP REQUIRES ACTION

If we sit around doing and saying nothing, little will happen. Inspiration and mobilization, the cornerstones of leadership, cannot happen without action. If we don't talk when we need to, we cannot lead. If we don't act when we need to, we cannot lead.

When we wish to exercise leadership, we need to express our ideas in some way. We can talk about our initiatives and inspire people through our words, or we can decide to do something and inspire them through our deeds. Either way, leadership is not simply about having an idea. It's about communicating it and acting upon it. Unless it is communicated in some form, it cannot inspire and mobilize others, and it is not leadership.

For example, the Swedish environmental activist Greta Thunberg inspired the world when she skipped school every Friday to protest in front of the Swedish Parliament, calling for immediate action and policies related to climate change. Her deeds inspired students in countries throughout the world to follow in her footsteps and start the "Fridays For Future" movement.[11]

Action can also include conscious and purposeful silence and stillness. Although this appears contradictory, the choice to remain silent and/or inactive can be immensely powerful if it is purposeful.

Reflection

After reading this article and considering the actions of Greta Thunberg, think of someone else who acted in a way that highlights this aspect of leadership. What lessons can you, or those close to you, learn from this person or group? How might you implement leadership in this form?

ACTION TIP:

Every day you should ask yourself: what did I do or say today to mobilize and inspire? Nothing will happen until somebody actually does something, so ensure you are being pro-active and responsive, and hold yourself accountable.

LEADERSHIP MANTRA

I will ensure that I am pro-active enough to see my purposeful ideas realized.

For your notes:

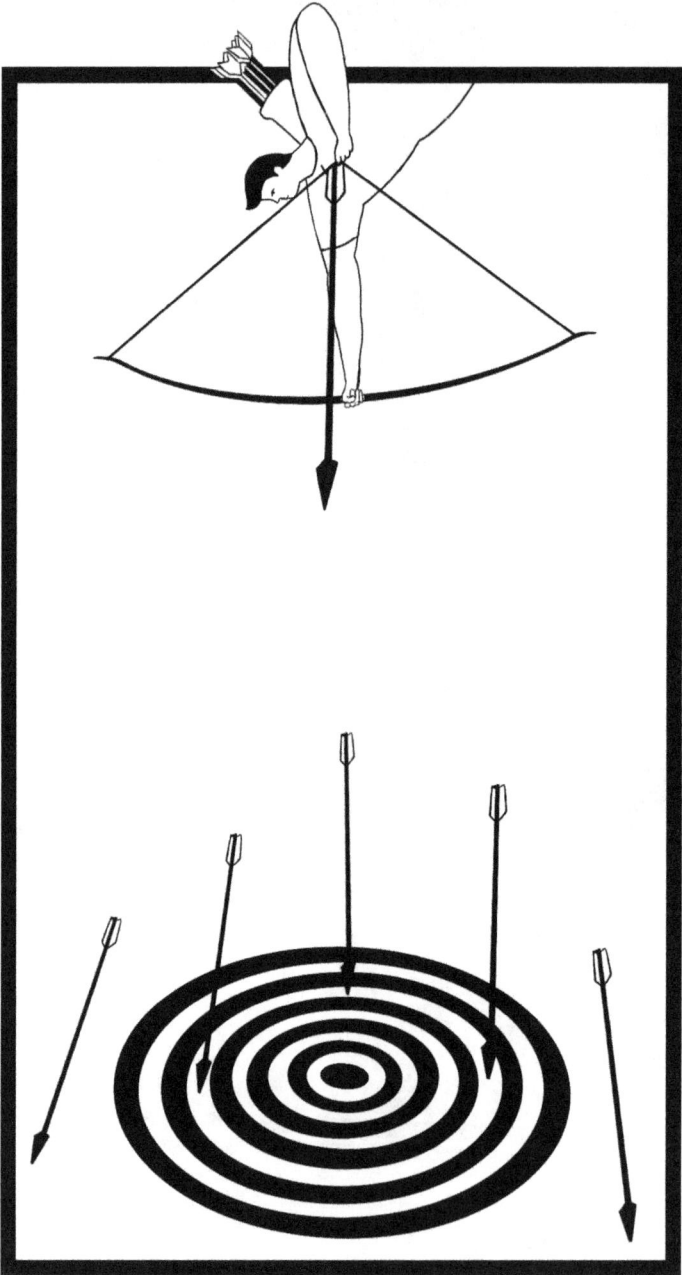

LEADERSHIP IS A STORY OF FAILURES

Failures in leadership are like the rungs of a ladder. To get to our destinations, we have no choice but to take every step and use it to progress. Good leadership is not determined solely by its successes.

This is not surprising when we consider how difficult leadership can be. Everyone involved will have their own issues, challenges, and perspectives to account for, and inspiring humans to embrace change and endure hardships for uncertain gain is a feat in itself. Add to this the unpredictable levels of resistance we must deal with, and the unexpected obstacles which we might encounter, and it is evident why failure is an integral part of leadership.

However, an act of leadership which fails to achieve its objective can still be a brilliant intervention. It may pave the way for other leadership initiatives to succeed, and it may sow the seeds of hope in those being mobilized so they themselves may eventually lead positive change.

There are times when we may introduce a leadership initiative even when we know in advance that it will fail (e.g. the resistance to it is too strong), because it is a necessary step on the ladder to success. Somebody trying, even if they fail, can encourage others to reexamine the status quo and think about whether they can bring their own initiatives forwards to improve it.

Consider the many countries throughout history which have worked to liberate themselves from occupation. In some instances, different people over a span of years will have attempted to mobilize the masses for rebellion. Many of these attempts failed to even mobilize, while many others were crushed under the immense force of the occupying nation. However, these attempts often inspired the ones which would then succeed. This is true of the USA's fight for independence from the British Empire, and for the countries that regained their independence during or after World War II.

In the end, the glory of success comes from enduring the failures that led to it. Be prepared to embrace failure and see it as part of your success.

ACTION TIP:

Nobody gets things right all the time. When you feel discouraged about your intervention, return to this section and remind yourself that failure is an integral part of leadership. Leading requires you to be resilient when it comes to failure, and to accept it as part of progress. Return to your sense of purpose if you feel discouraged and need motivation.

LEADERSHIP MANTRA

Our cause is worth failing for.

Leadership is ...

An adventure.

LEADERSHIP IS SOMETIMES ABOUT BEING A GOOD FOLLOWER

Leadership is not about us, but about the purpose we are mobilizing for. Sometimes, the best idea or intervention will not be our own. In such situations, the best act of leadership is to recognize this, support the person whose initiative is better, and mobilize others towards that idea. This is one instance where we can inspire, motivate, and mobilize simply by being great followers.

Sometimes, leadership can be exercised by asking the questions that will encourage people to think carefully about their lives and their options. Without necessarily having the answers ourselves, we can open up the stage for ideas to emerge from different people – possibly including some who have a better mobilizing capacity than us. They may then take the lead and help the group move forward.

It does not matter whose initiative benefits the system and its constituents. Remember, leadership is about helping the system's constituents live in fulfillment and dignity. If someone has an initiative that will help the system progress, embrace and follow it. It is through our acceptance and "following" that others may also be inspired to follow.

To sum this idea up:

My way… your way… it doesn't matter. Is it going to benefit us? Yes? Great, let's go.

"He who cannot be a good follower cannot be a good leader."

– Aristotle

ACTION TIP:

Make a habit of reminding yourself that your initiative is not about you. This will help you support others if their initiative is stronger than yours. Remember that supporting an initiative inspires others to believe in it, and will also increase people's trust in your motivation when it comes to your own initiative; they will have seen that you are not self-serving, but are trying to improve the system.

LEADERSHIP MANTRA

I will follow and support any person or idea that will lead to a better future.

For your notes:

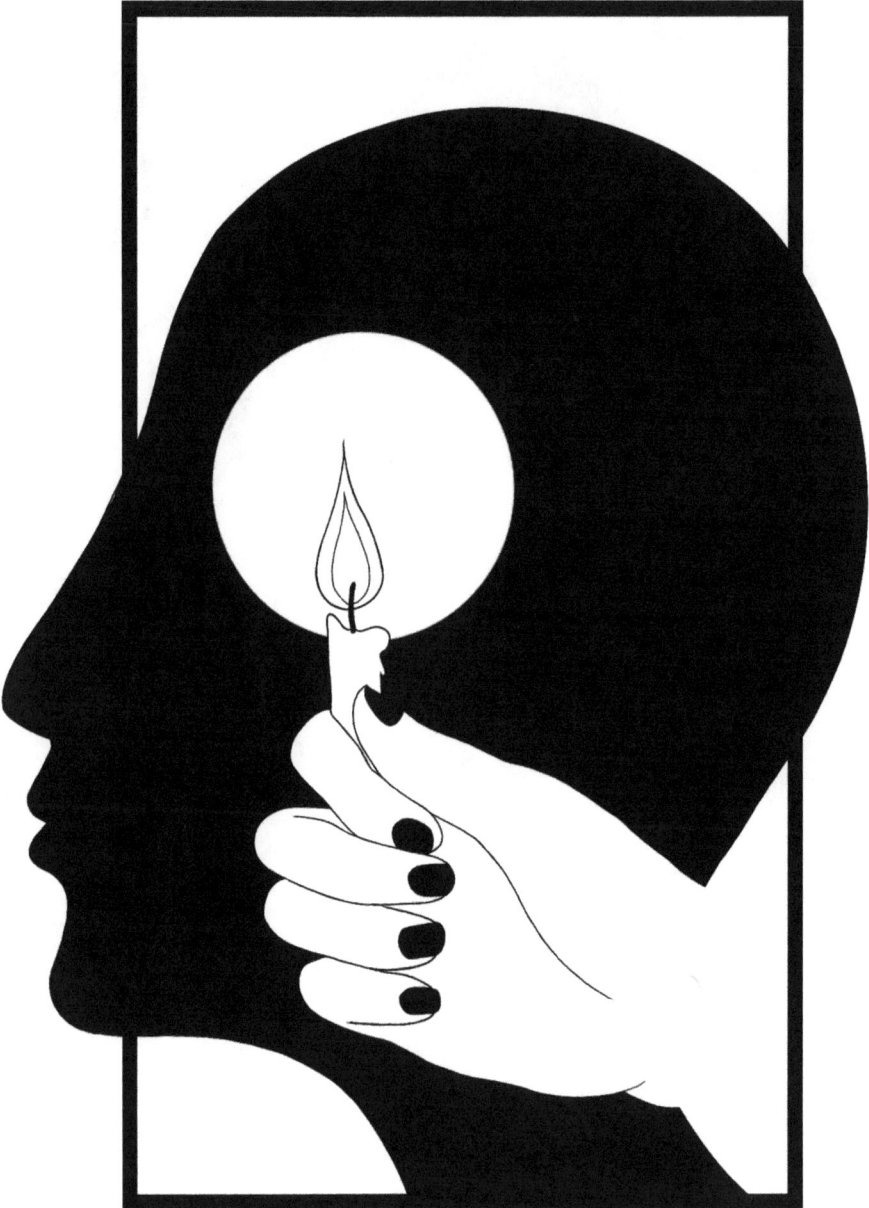

LEADERSHIP BREEDS HOPE

One of the primary duties of leadership is to instill people with the hope that the future could be better, even if people and organizations are in a state of despair. Hope comes easily when there is an optimistic atmosphere, but it is equally necessary – perhaps even more so – when there is a sense of pessimism, and everything seems negative. When the general attitude is subdued, putting energy into a purposeful initiative may seem futile, so it's important to spark enthusiasm for the future.

Leadership is about promoting hope, even if the majority believes that there is no hope.

For instance, almost every colony that ever moved against the occupying empire started with people spreading hope that one day the country would gain its independence. No war for independence was ever launched without the hope of freedom being planted in people's minds and hearts. Of course, the rebels did not have any guarantees, and some of them might have even witnessed failed attempts to overthrow the occupation, but many persevered because they still hoped for a better future.

Let us consider another group where hope played a crucial role in their survival: prisoners of war. The atrocities endured by prisoners of war would make many of us flinch and shudder. However, as the renowned psychiatrist Viktor Frankl mentioned, it was often those who had purpose, meaning, and hope of a better future – who had something to live for – that made it through those difficult times. Those who did not have hope, on the other hand, gave up, and many of them wasted away and died before their freedom could be restored.[12]

Leadership starts with hope. If there was no hope, why would people sacrifice and give up certainty, comfort, and routine? Hope allows people to take a leap of faith, to believe that enduring the pain and loss will be worthwhile.

Leadership should build people's faith in the creative capacity of the group, in their resilience, in their buoyancy, and in their successful history of dealing with challenges. This will bolster their endurance and increase their willingness to keep trying, work collectively, and come up with creative solutions.

Leadership boldly states that "Hope is always available; especially in a state of desperation and hopelessness."

ACTION TIP:

Crystallize in your own mind what your initiative hopes to achieve, and then convey this idea to others. Always try to ensure that your words and actions are positive and reflect your belief that the future can and will be better. Try to get people to associate you and your initiative with hope for the future.

LEADERSHIP MANTRA

*I will try to plant hope in the hearts of everyone
I meet.*

LEADERSHIP IS SOMETIMES SOLELY FOCUSED ON STAYING ALIVE AND FUNCTIONAL

Although most of the time leadership is about mobilizing people or groups to create progress and focus on growth, sometimes survival is threatened, and this is where leadership needs to focus. At times, we may need to consider introducing initiatives that aim to keep people, groups, or organizations alive, while minimizing damage, reducing pain and loss, and/or preventing panic.

It takes great skill to pilot an airplane full of passengers in a perfectly smooth flight when the conditions are favorable. However, it takes even greater skill to safely land an aircraft, with its passengers, when there are difficult weather conditions or technical failures. In this case, brilliance is not about the smoothness of the flight, but about a safe landing.

In the corporate world, sometimes great leadership is about keeping the company afloat or reducing its losses when the economy is in a state of depression.

The former mayor of New York City, Rudy Giuliani, received

more praise for his leadership skills in the wake of 9/11 than he had ever done before. His ability to act quickly and unite the people of New York amid an unprecedented and horrendous crisis earned him much admiration – he was named TIME Magazine Person of the Year.[13]

That is why leadership is not always about sustaining a momentum of growth. Sometimes it is about minimizing losses, and helping people survive in the face of abrupt change.

ACTION TIP:

When the environment is threatening your (or your group's) survival, focus on minimizing damage in any way you can. Make a list of the dangers and how you can most effectively negate them. Be aware of who is at risk, and try to protect them where possible.

LEADERSHIP MANTRA

There will be times where the best we can do is survive. That's life. We will survive so that soon we can grow again.

For your notes:

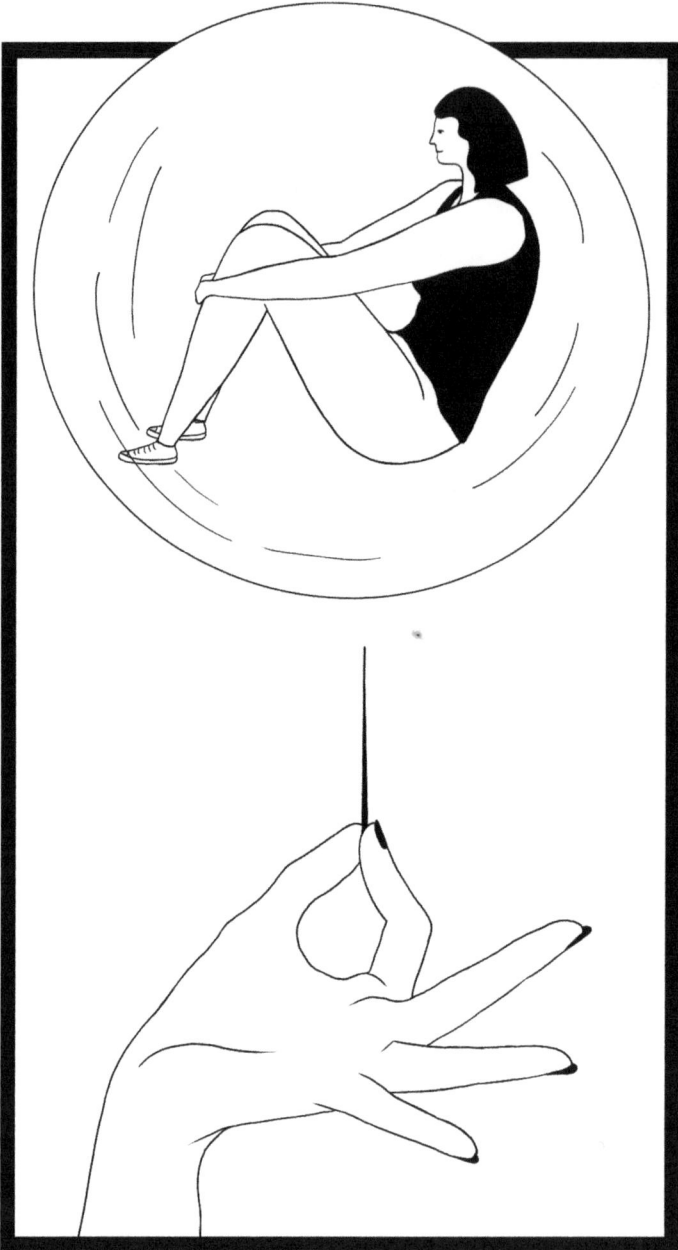

LEADERSHIP IS ABOUT CREATING PURPOSEFUL CHAOS AND STRATEGIC INSTABILITY

Leadership sometimes demands consciously, strategically, and deliberately creating calculated disequilibrium to push people out of their comfort zones. This will encourage them to start exploring and learning, and help them develop their strengths, character, and resilience. Ultimately, building people's strengths will help them deal with life's difficulties and create or capture new opportunities.

Think of this like growing up: as children, we depend on adults to do everything for us, but as we grow, we assume increasing responsibilities, and learn the skills necessary to fulfill these responsibilities. This often involves discomfort and facing the unknown, but without it, we would remain dependent on others forever. Some of these learning moments may feel chaotic, but they are essential for growth.

With children, it is relatively easy to encourage them out of their comfort zones; we can do so in a controlled way, mitigate any pain, offer support, and preempt problems. Children are also often more willing to try something new.

With adults, it is more complicated because they are usually more firmly rooted in their comfort zones, and it is harder to implement controlled chaos. This is also the case for introducing chaos to complicated systems such as businesses, communities, and particularly entire countries. The more complex the system, the trickier it is to manage chaos. There are many moving parts, which makes it hard to predict how things will pan out, and increases the chance of something going wrong.

When we "rock the boat," we might succeed in creating disequilibrium, but, if we aren't controlling the movement to a degree (especially in complex systems like conglomerates and countries), the boat might capsize.

Not considering the impacts of chaos or failing to handle it with care can destroy entire systems. Leadership must seek only strategic chaos, pushing people out of their comfort zones without capsizing their system.

This is extremely delicate and requires experienced leadership skills, and it has to be done with care, attention, careful understanding, and humility.

ACTION TIP:

When you see your people becoming passive and too relaxed, encourage them to take on challenges which will sharpen their survival instincts and their creative thinking. Be careful not to create uncontrollable chaos and hurt people instead of helping them.

LEADERSHIP MANTRA

Continuous babysitting keeps people like babies.

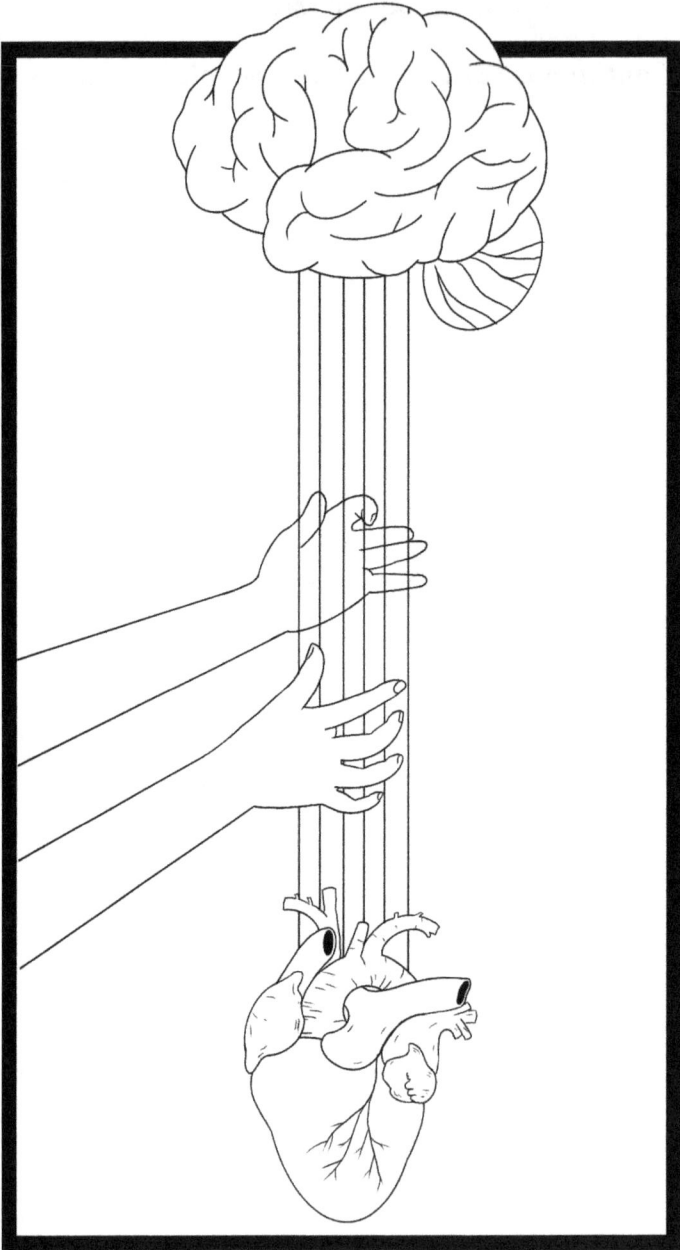

LEADERSHIP ADDRESSES MINDS, HEARTS, AND SOULS

Leadership is about addressing the mind, heart, and soul. Since leadership is about mobilizing people, it must address each dimension of a human being's psyche.

Leadership addresses the **mind** because our ideas must make sense to the people we are mobilizing. If an initiative does not seem well thought out, people will be less willing to support it. We need to know how to convey the rationality and logic of our plans so people can understand *why* they should accept them.

It addresses the **heart** because we are emotional beings. If we fail to mobilize people's hearts, they will lack enthusiasm, and our mobilization efforts may suffer. Remember also that leadership initiatives will spark many emotions, from excitement to fear to anger. We must respect and anticipate these responses.

It addresses the **soul**, focusing on what people value and what they consider to be moral. If we don't take these things into account, we will be unable to ensure that our initiatives respect ethical boundaries. People need to know that an initiative is not only beneficial, but that it does not compromise their values.

When we mobilize, we should consider all three, because if we fail to address any of them, this will create resistance and hinder our progress.

Let us look at some of the ways in which people who exercised great leadership successfully appealed to the minds, hearts, and values of the people they were mobilizing, starting with the famous speech that Susan B. Anthony – who was a major player in the suffrage movement in the United States – gave after she was charged with illegally casting her vote at a time when women were barred from voting.[14]

She addressed her listeners' minds by making references to the constitution and well-respected and credible dictionaries. "It was we, the people; not we, the white male citizens; nor yet we, the male citizens; but we, the whole people, who formed the Union."

Her speech then explored the constitutional values, appealing to her audience's souls. "And we formed it, not to give the blessings of liberty, but to secure them; not to the half of ourselves and the half of our posterity, but to the whole people – women as well as men."

She later addressed her listeners' hearts by showing them how denying women their right to vote would create issues within every family. "This oligarchy of sex, which makes father, brothers, husband, sons, the oligarchs over the mother and sisters, the wife and daughters of every household – which ordains all men sovereigns, all women subjects, carries dissension, discord and rebellion into every home of the nation."[15]

The same pattern applies to two other famous speeches: Abraham Lincoln's "Gettysburg Address" and Dr. Martin Luther King Jr.'s "I Have A Dream."

Let us consider the Gettysburg Address. By reciting history of the nation and its creed, Lincoln addressed the soldiers' minds and souls: "Four score and seven years ago our fathers brought forth, upon this continent, a new nation, conceived in liberty, and dedicated to the proposition that all men are created equal."

By recognizing the tireless efforts of the "brave" soldiers and the lives lost on the battlefield, he addressed his listeners' hearts: "The brave men, living and dead, who struggled here, have consecrated it far above our poor power to add or detract. The world will little note, nor long remember what we say here, but it can never forget what they did here."[16]

One hundred years later, Martin Luther King Jr. inspired a nation in 1963 as he stood on the steps of the Lincoln Memorial and delivered the iconic speech that moved the hearts, minds, and souls of his listeners. He addressed their minds and souls by citing the constitution and pointing out that despite the constitutional right of every citizen to be treated equally, people of color were still not afforded their rights. He went on to describe his powerful dream of a world free from racial injustice and segregation, moving his audience's hearts as they imagined Dr. King's dream coming true.[17]

Remember, acts of leadership are not reserved solely for speeches or nationwide movements. They can happen on smaller scales, and even on an individual level. Whenever we introduce acts of leadership that come from an authentic, compassionate, just, purposeful, and loving place, it will often target the minds, hearts, and souls of those being mobilized.

Reflection

Take a moment to consider other people who gave moving speeches, or whose actions spoke to people's minds, hearts, and souls.

- Did their mobilization attempts have a beneficial purpose?
- If so, would you count them as acts of leadership?
- What have you learned from them?
- How have you applied what they taught you to your own life?
- What changes have you made because of what this person or group said or did?
- Did you then try to mobilize others to do the same? How?

Recall, as well, a time in your life when your actions spoke to people's minds, hearts, and souls. You may have exercised leadership without realizing it.

ACTION TIP:

Think about how you can structure your initiative around these three areas. Make sure you are not only communicating through logical channels, but that you are also responding to people's values and to their emotions. Write down things that you think will be important to others for each category, and plan your approach accordingly. You can even do this when persuading yourself to an action; don't just look at it from a logical perspective, but engage your emotions and sense of morality as well.

LEADERSHIP MANTRA

In everything I do or say, I will seek to touch my people's souls, hearts, and minds.

Leadership is...

About doing good. It's an act of love – which is what the world NEEDS.

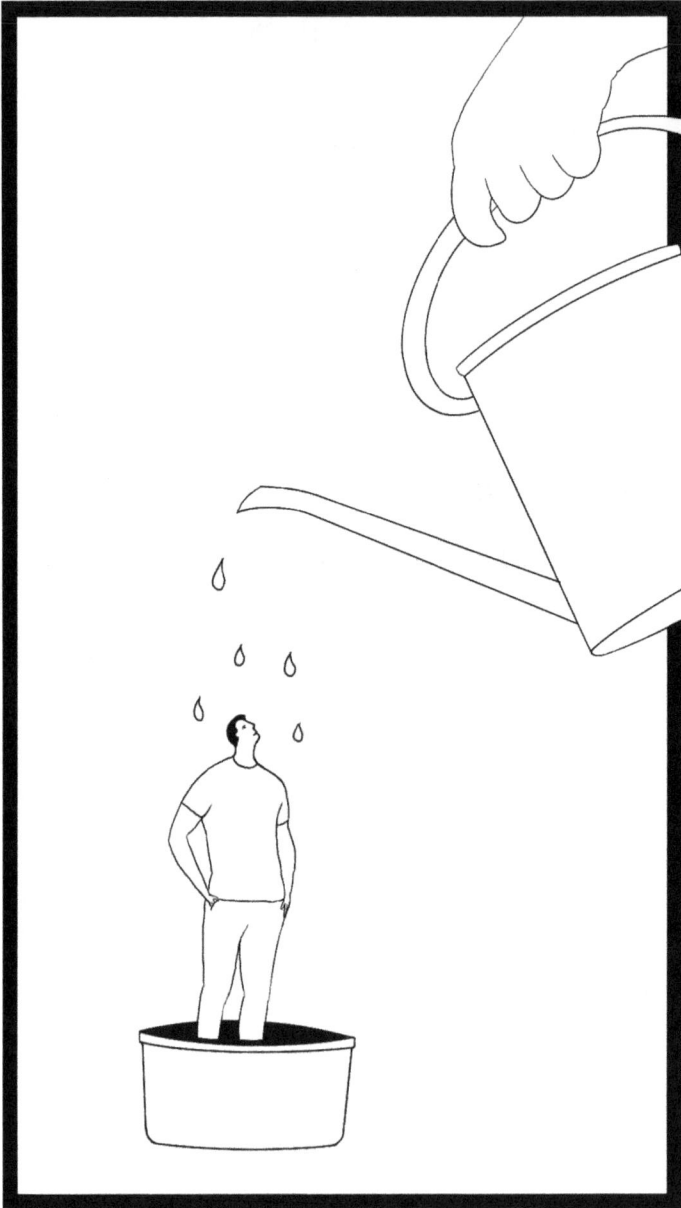

LEADERSHIP CREATES AN ENVIRONMENT WHERE OTHER LEADERS EMERGE

Remember that leadership is about mobilizing individuals to hone their capacities and reach their full potential. The greatest form of leadership is one that creates an environment which allows other leaders to emerge. This is an environment where people feel hopeful, important, and confident enough in their own abilities to be a catalyst for change.

The mark of strong leadership is that it empowers members of the group to exercise successful self-leadership. For the individuals or groups to change, transform, and grow, each member of the system must grow through self-leadership.

Max Tegmark, an MIT professor, co-founded the Future of Life Institute to start a joint conversation about Artificial Intelligence (AI) among prominent scientists and tech entrepreneurs and researchers. His work aims to increase awareness about the benefits and setbacks of developing AIs. His initiative led to a growing network of tens of thousands of individuals working together to consciously consider the guidelines and principles that are necessary to develop a benevolent AI. This conversation has helped inspire others to mobilize people in their respective fields and create organizations that are working towards the same purpose.[18]

ACTION TIP:

Whenever you see an opportunity to promote leadership, take it. Move others from being spectators to being players. Either invite people to join you in carrying your burden of leadership, or encourage them to implement their own ideas to contribute to the journey of growth. Support other initiatives whenever you can, ensuring other leaders are empowered and encouraged.

LEADERSHIP MANTRA

My role is to evoke the greatness that lies within us all.

When people tell you "Thank you," let it sink in, and take a few moments to remind yourself of the goodness that is within you.

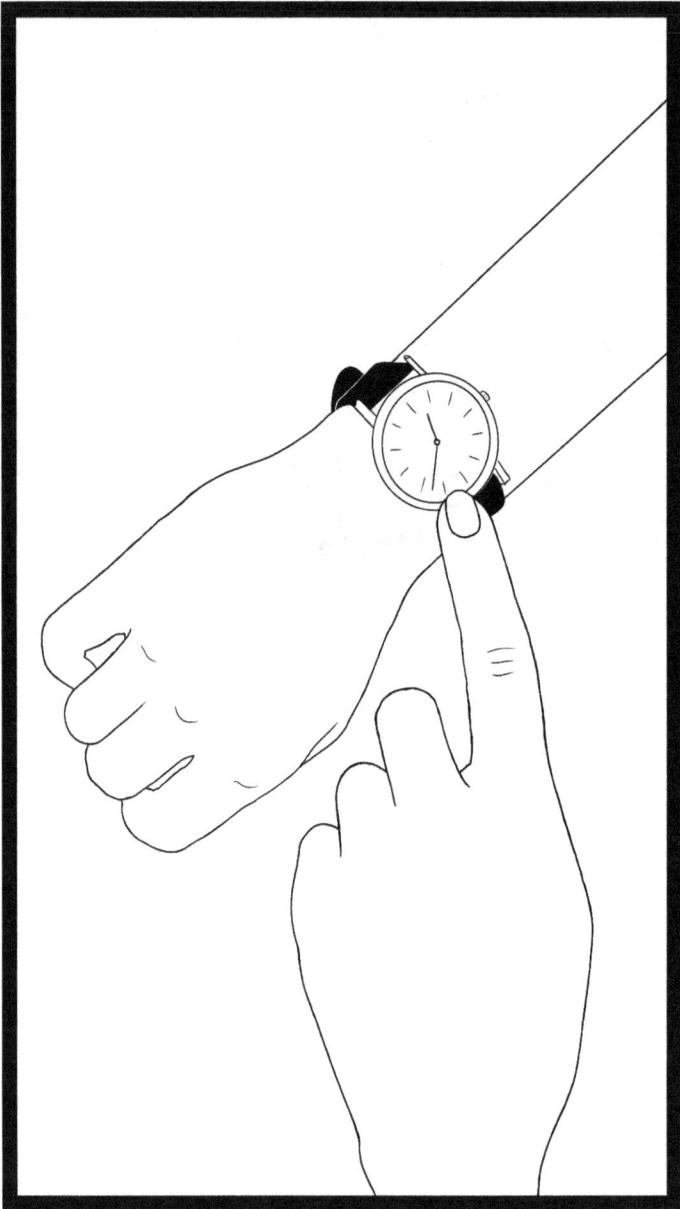

LEADERSHIP KNOWS WHAT IS IMPORTANT NOW

A key component of leadership is prioritization, and this hinges on understanding the environment in which we are introducing change. Leadership is about accurately diagnosing the challenges and identifying the opportunities available in the current reality.

Knowing what is important at any particular time is a basic requirement if we want to effectively manage our energies and resources in the general journey of survival and growth. We need to know what to focus on, and how much of ourselves we should devote to it.

This is crucial to leadership whether:

1. We and those we are mobilizing need to deal with a challenge or problem.

2. There is an opportunity for growth that we and those we are mobilizing need to capture.

If we exhaust ourselves before we are able to deal with a challenge or capture an opportunity, our leadership initiatives may fail.

As the ones exercising leadership, we must be able to distinguish between things that are unimportant, things that are reasonably important, and things that are crucially important. This means assessing opportunities and threats, carefully planning the distribution of our resources, and remaining adaptive, since circumstances beyond our control could change at any time.

When a crisis happens, it becomes the priority, and we will have to allocate most of our resources and energies to resolving it. As an example of this, consider how presidents and heads of state might cancel a diplomatic visit to a foreign country if there was a crisis in their own country (e.g. natural disasters, security threats, etc.). This new development would shift their priorities, and they would need to devote their time, effort, and resources to the crisis.

An act of leadership requires adaptation and sound judgment at every significant moment to determine what's important now, what can wait, and what is not important at all. As the ones exercising leadership, we do not have time to waste. If we constantly focus on things that are not important then the challenges that we need to face may magnify, and we will find ourselves failing, as well as causing others pain because of failures we could have possibly avoided.

ACTION TIP:

To apply this in a practical sense, make sure you frequently remind yourself of:
- The purpose of your leadership act.
- Your top priorities for achieving this purpose in the long-term.
- What is important at the present moment of the journey.

If necessary, write down key things which you need to achieve, and log the required resources alongside. This will ensure you are focused and effectively distributing your resources.

LEADERSHIP MANTRA

I am aware of my priorities in every moment and every situation.

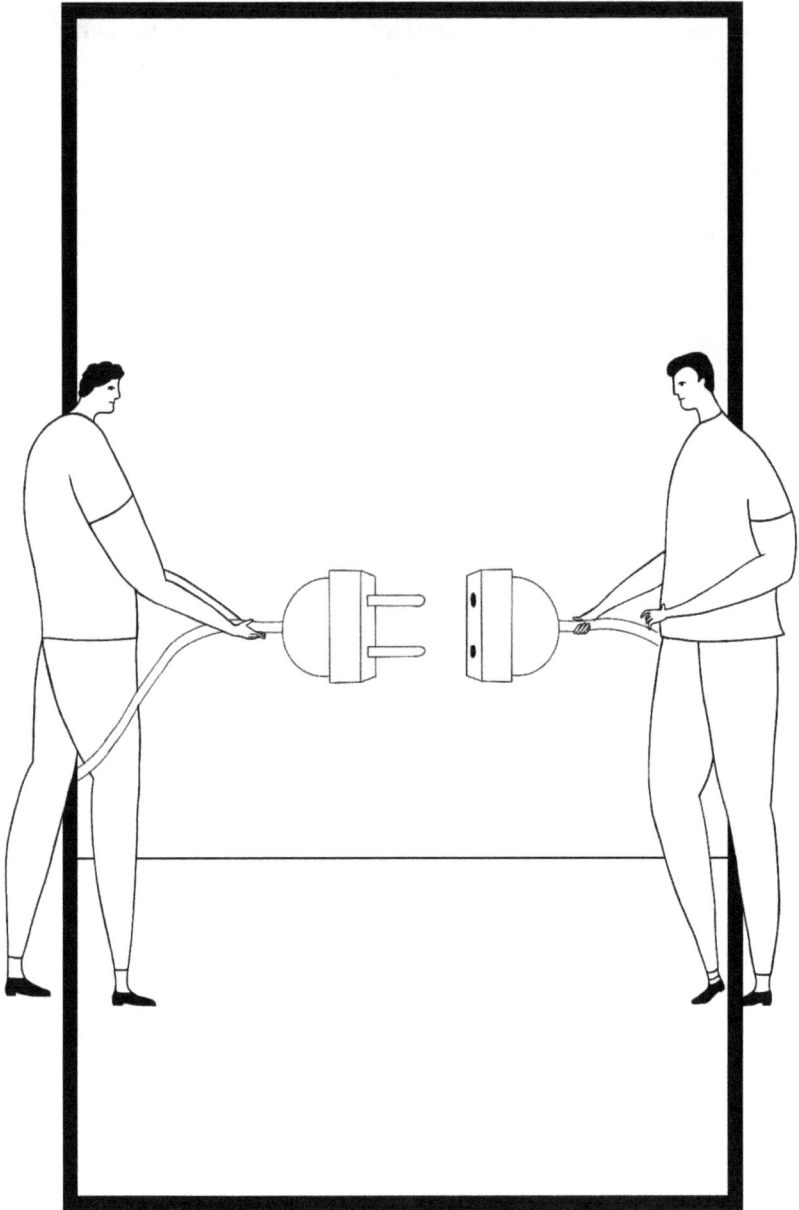

LEADERSHIP ALMOST ALWAYS REQUIRES MAKING A CONNECTION

It is only through connections that leadership is exercised, because there is no mobilization without connection.

It is through connection that one can exercise empathy and listen to people's hopes, pains, fears, ideas, and aspirations. When we invest time into connections, we will understand who we are mobilizing, and that includes understanding their reality. This will allow us to frame the approach of our initiative to suit their perspective, to personalize it and make it relatable. We will also be able to point out opportunities or future benefits which they may have overlooked. All this will solidify their understanding of the current reality and increase their hopes, and by extension their willingness to embrace change for the sake of living a more fulfilled and beautiful life.

In addition, the person exercising leadership should try to understand the objections which people may have about their intervention; some may be valid and require attention, and all should be recognized. Hearing different perspectives may lead to adjustments in the plan, which may make the change more beneficial, and could reduce the resistance to it.

Remember, we need to address the minds, hearts, and souls of individuals if we wish to successfully mobilize and lead them. We cannot hope to do that if we do not take the time to build a connection with them.

ACTION TIP:

Take every opportunity to connect with others, both within and outside of the initiative. Bond with people, get to know them, and take opportunities to build a relationship. This will help you to inspire and mobilize them, because you will have laid a foundation of trust, and you will better understand how to help people.

LEADERSHIP MANTRA

I will strive to make deep, authentic connections with people in the world around me.

Exercising leadership will...

Give our lives profound depth, and
a sense of meaning that we will not
find in other areas of our lives.

LEADERSHIP IS AT TIMES A LONELY ENTERPRISE

Leadership can often be lonely. When the challenges are serious and the pressure is high, we may find ourselves questioning whether it is all worth it. In those moments of fear and skepticism, we will feel like we are alone. Our own doubts may make us fear the doubts of others.

The resistance we are likely to experience from some may push others away, even if they initially supported us. Others may abandon the initiative mid-journey. Others still may continue to support us, but with skepticism. It is not uncommon for a person exercising leadership to find that even their closest allies and most passionate supporters have abandoned them and their initiative.

It is in these difficult moments of solitude that we must stay the course in this lonely journey so that we can inspire courage, resilience, and steadfastness in others, even when we ourselves are terrified.

CEOs, presidents, and social reformers know how lonely it is on the top. Most people look to us for reassurance and answers, and being unable to comfort them can be hard. It is equally difficult to avoid sharing our own doubts, insecurities, and fears. Sometimes it is necessary to keep these to ourselves to avoid panicking others in the system. In that sense, leadership is lonely.

Having said that, it is naïve to think that the daunting task of mobilizing others on a difficult journey can be successful when undertaken alone – it is almost impossible for someone to withstand that kind of pressure without some support.

Prophets, great historical figures, CEOs, and even athletes have all faced great pressure and temporary loneliness, but it is important to remember that they have rarely triumphed without support.

ACTION TIP:

Prepare for moments of loneliness. If nobody within the system is supportive, keep moving forward, but don't isolate yourself. Look for confidants unrelated to the initiative to whom you can express your emotions and thoughts. They will help you process them so that they do not overwhelm you.

Surround yourself with a strong support structure, which could come from family or friends. Make time for other social activities that will take you away from the politics of your initiative, and give you an opportunity to spend pleasant time with others.

LEADERSHIP MANTRA

I know that sometimes I will feel lonely, and that's okay. I will stay the course.

For your notes:

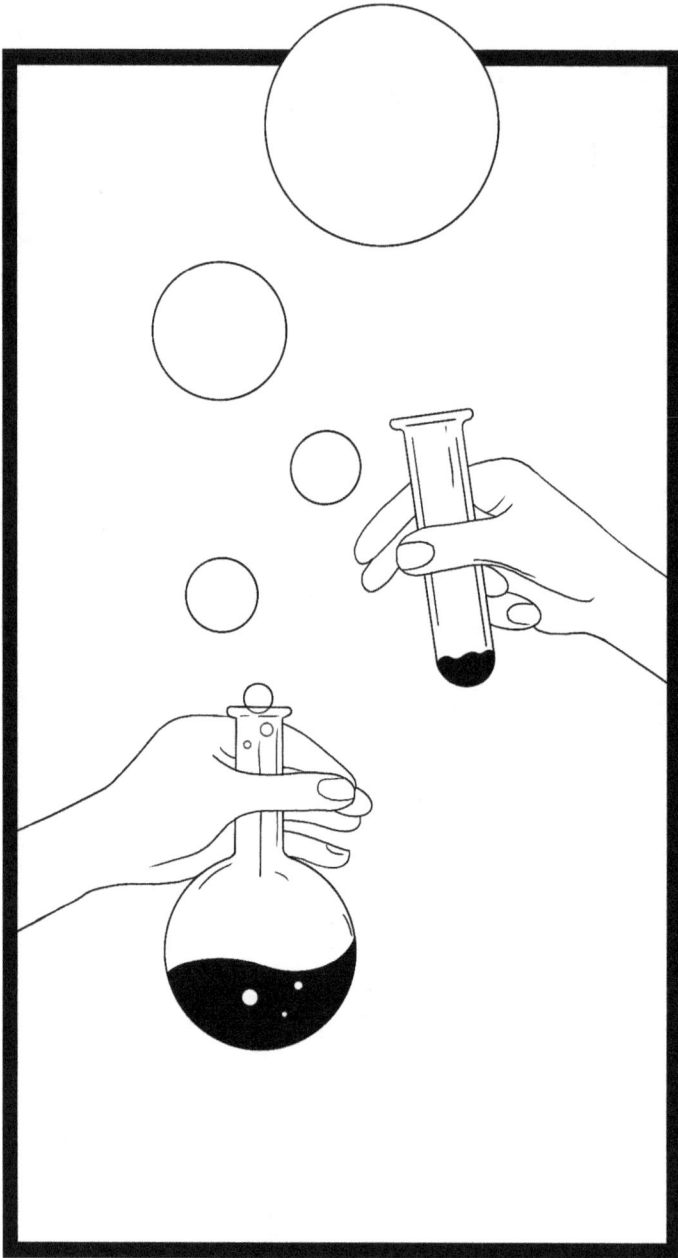

LEADERSHIP DEMANDS EXPERIMENTATION

The fact that the future is unpredictable means that when we are exercising leadership, we will often explore new terrain. We may encounter problems along the way that we will not fully understand. We will need to examine these problems from different angles, and look for creative solutions.

We may encounter situations that are not new, which already have tried-and-tested solutions. Solving such situations is often a job for authority or an expert. They will apply known methods and solutions to resolve an "old" issue. Of course, sometimes the context will have changed, and an "old" problem will require a "new" solution, which means that exercising leadership is actually needed. In fact, part of remaining adaptive means tackling old issues by experimenting with new and possibly improved methods.

In other cases, the situation will be completely novel, possibly unexpected, and this also calls for leadership. We will have to resort to trial and error, testing out various creative solutions. Some of the solutions will resolve the problem immediately, but other problems will prove more difficult. We will fail to resolve them a few times before we develop a functional way of successfully dealing with a totally new reality. Leadership is messy because it is often accompanied by bouts of failed experimentation.

In 1933, amid the Great Depression, Franklin D. Roosevelt became president. With an unprecedented challenge ahead of him (bringing an end to the Great Depression) he spent the first two terms of his presidency (8 years) experimenting with different federal programs. Although most of the programs he introduced were overturned or abandoned, they restored hope and vivacity to his country.[19] He was willing to experiment with what many in his administration disapproved of, and to mobilize his country towards progress. His initiatives were unquestionably acts of leadership.

Of course, sometimes a problem may prove too complex, or the pressures that it presents are too great. If we are stuck, we must be willing to let go temporarily. When we have come up with new strategies to tackle the problem, then we go back and give it another shot.

ACTION TIP:

Make sure you are branching out from the tried-and-tested methods and applying new, creative solutions to problems. Remember that art is often the result of experimentation, of 'trying' new things – make sure you try. If something doesn't work, look at why it didn't work, and try something different.

LEADERSHIP MANTRA

We will keep trying until we get it right. Getting it wrong is just another opportunity to learn how to get it right.

In addition to economic abundance,
leadership must have...

A moral, social and spiritual dimension, so
that people can experience healthy and
holistic growth.

LEADERSHIP NEEDS IMPROVISATION

I disagree with the analogy that compares leadership with conducting an orchestra. While this image may describe some aspects of authority, leadership is more of an act of improvisation than an act of control and coordination.

In the case of the maestro, the musical piece is complete and known to him/her. S/he has full control over the orchestra. The musicians are skilled, know their parts well, and are totally loyal to the conductor.

In this case, the probable outcome is clear. The orchestra, under the direction of the maestro, will play the musical piece in a skilled and masterful manner.

The reality of leadership is not the same. The person exercising leadership does not know the exact future, s/he may not have any control over the system, and even if s/he has some control, it is unlikely to be the same type of control a maestro has. The "players" may not be loyal, may not follow and embrace what the person exercising leadership is proposing, and may not know their "parts" in bringing about purposeful change.

The person exercising leadership does not have access to the same level of information that a maestro has. The music might change, or there might not be any music to play, so the person exercising leadership needs to improvise and come up with something to keep the audience engaged and move the performance forward.

While the skills required of a conductor are valuable, leadership often demands a wider variety of skills, as it needs to handle problems that are new to everybody, including the "conductor" him/herself.

For example, in normal conditions, the minister of health knows how to deal with the everyday routines of healthcare. She, like the conductor, can operate her entire apparatus – hospitals, doctors, medications, etc. – to deal with the usual and expected health issues of the country. In the case of a sudden outbreak of a new disease, without a known treatment, the rules of the game shift. The minister cannot behave as if it is "business as usual." She will need to improvise, and try new things to deal with the situation. Instead of conducting, she must lead.

Therefore, leadership is, to a great extent, about improvisation. It involves failure, listening to different perspectives, and not knowing what to do. It lacks any guarantees about how the situation will develop. It echoes part of the reality of life in terms of uncertainty, unpredictability, unexpected surprises, and miscalculated plans and strategies.

ACTION TIP:

Keep your plans flexible, and don't allow negativity to creep in if something goes awry. You may have to keep improvising and trying new things over and over again; accept this as part of the challenges of leadership, and move forward. Remember that while you remain committed to your purpose, you will need to maintain an adaptive strategy, to accommodate for the changes in your environment.

LEADERSHIP MANTRA

*I will think of something. I always find a way when
I am focused and authentic.*

LEADERSHIP CREATES ABUNDANCE AND PROSPERITY

Leadership is about creating an abundance of the things which make people's lives positive – opportunities, love, food, health, empathy, etc. This can be at work, at home, in an organization, or on a wider scale.

Consider this in terms of survival and growth. Only by creating abundance can we secure our survival. When we have everything we need, we feel safe and secure. We no longer have to worry about risking our lives, and we can focus less on survival and more on growth. When we, as the ones exercising leadership, provide abundance, those we are mobilizing can choose how best to elevate their own lives.

A person exercising leadership attempts to create an environment that:

- Offers an abundance of sustenance, natural resources, shelter, and safety.

- Encourages relationships with others and with nature.

- Grants opportunities for people to build social presence and allows them to expand their support systems.

- Inspires healthy emotional expression, emotional acceptance, and strategies for dealing with destructive or unwanted feelings.

- Secures a wealth of opportunities for spiritual and religious expression so that people may satisfy their spiritual side.

- Offers an abundance of materials and opportunities for people to create and apply their ideas to keep growing.

In the corporate world, leadership is about creating sustainable financial growth, about building and protecting market share, customer loyalty, a good reputation, etc., and about fulfilling the organization's purpose by making a valuable contribution to its clients.

Great leadership also takes on the responsibility of creating various forms of abundance in the lives of the organization's employees and their families. This act is one of the highest forms of service that an organization can do, because if an organization doesn't care for and do good for its employees, who operate it, then how can it do genuine good to the customers, who are outsiders? People are people, whether they work for the organization or are its customers. Double standards in treating them cannot be the hallmark of authentic leadership.

In the public domain, it is about creating a flourishing economy that provides job opportunities, increases the standard of living, and generally elevates the quality of life.

Leadership is about creating an environment where people will flourish and fulfill their personal purposes, and have an enriched and meaningful experience of life.

The ultimate purpose of leadership is to help people endure the hardships of life, and enhance their experience of meaningful living.

ACTION TIP:

Frequently do an audit of the results of your leadership initiatives. If abundance is not being created when it should be, you need to examine what is going on and redirect the course. Identify what areas you are trying to create abundance in so you can clearly see whether you are succeeding or not.

LEADERSHIP MANTRA

My purpose is to create a life of abundance, prosperity, meaning, and fulfillment.

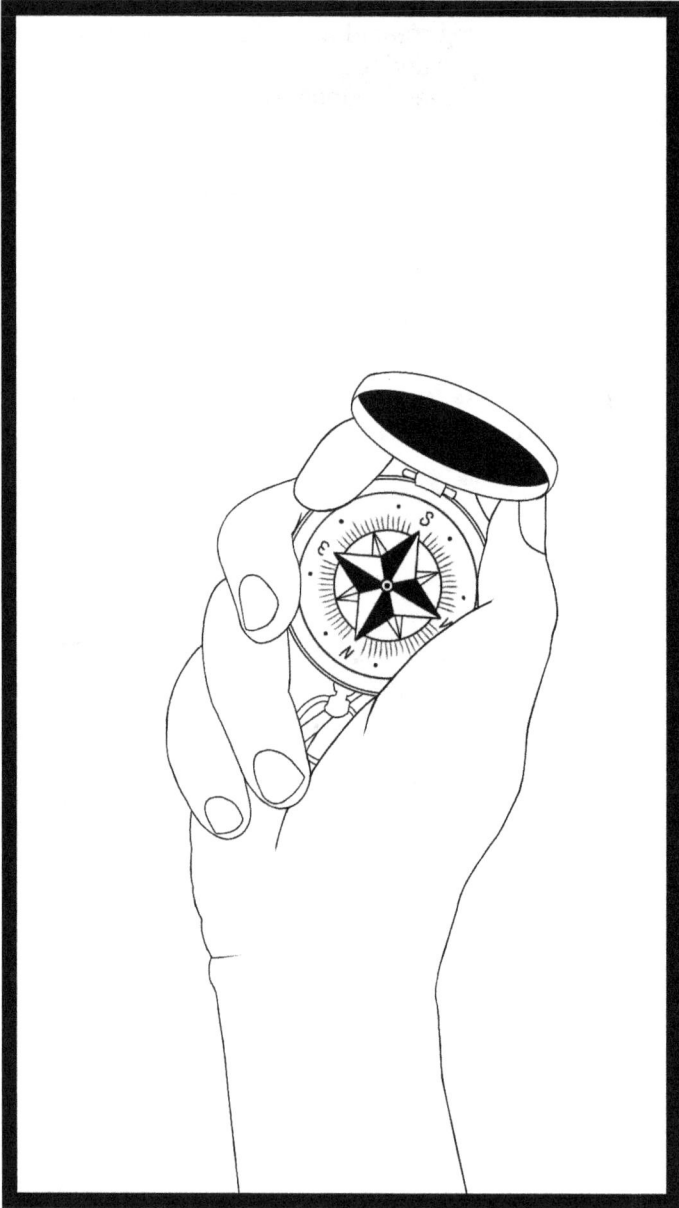

LEADERSHIP OFTEN HAS A GENERAL SENSE OF DIRECTION RATHER THAN AN ACCURATE VISION OF THE FUTURE

Remember that life is in constant flux, and there will be times when the person exercising leadership does not know how to progress. To suggest that a "leader" knows exactly what the future will look like in a highly unpredictable world can be a little pretentious. Nobody knows the future, nobody has all the answers, and leadership does not ask this of anyone.

However, as the ones exercising leadership, we will have a sense of which way to "go." To exercise leadership, a person must have some concept of how reality could be better. Purpose will help us find this sense of direction and remain adaptive as we exercise leadership. It will help us ground the initiative in reality, ensuring that we are guiding others towards an improved future.

As Peter Drucker once said,

"The only thing we know about the future is that it will be different."

Let us compare exercising leadership to sailing. When a person sails to a chosen location, they know their general direction – they know where they want to end up. At times, they may have a specific route they have mapped out, but they cannot be certain of how the journey will actually unfold. They may not be able to accurately predict the weather or sea conditions, or the reliability of their equipment. They might experience a storm, underestimate the necessary supplies, experience technical failures, etc.

Exercising leadership is not contingent on planning the journey down to the last detail. People need to accept that they will often only have a general sense of where the endpoint of the initiative should be, and that they will need to be flexible as they deal with unexpected variables. A "leader's" job is to identify how the future could be better, and to start people moving in that direction.

ACTION TIP:

Remember that the future might not be the one you visualize. Be clear on the criteria that you need to achieve for the initiative to be a success, and be flexible about the other elements. In the sailing example, the criteria for success would be reaching the destination safely.

LEADERSHIP MANTRA

It's okay if the future is not absolutely clear. What's important is that we are moving in the right direction. We will eventually get there.

LEADERSHIP IS ABOUT FEELING RESPONSIBLE

Leadership is about feeling responsible even when we are not held responsible. Regardless of whether people are expecting us to lead or not, exercising leadership comes with an internal sense of responsibility. We feel that it is our ethical and moral duty to do our best to help others progress.

Leadership stems from caring about the lives of others. Sometimes, we do not exercise leadership because we have to, but because we feel it is our duty to do so. We will not be held accountable, except maybe to ourselves, if we do not exercise leadership, but it is embedded with a sense of moral obligation that prevents us from being passive in situations where others are stuck or living a suboptimal life. It is a voluntary sense of responsibility.

Leadership is needed when people fail to solve their problems, challenges, and issues, as well as when they fail to capture or create opportunities for growth and construct a better reality. People are stuck when they cannot do any of the above.

Have you ever wondered why we have unleaded gasoline? Or why in some places we are warned about leaded paint? Clair Patterson was a scientist who spent approximately 20 years researching lead, and showed that it was becoming extremely prevalent in our atmosphere, our oceans, our water, our homes, and our cities. The resistance he faced and the personal turmoil he went through would be reason enough for anyone to give up on such a challenging initiative. However, he felt it was his responsibility to bring attention to the dangers of this slow-working poison, which we were willingly injecting into our lives.

Despite resistance from the automotive industry and their partners, Clair Patterson persevered. With time and research, he was able to repeatedly show the danger of lead and its prevalence in our lives. His efforts mobilized different agencies in the United States to ban the use of lead in different products, including gasoline and paint.[20]

Clair Patterson took on responsibility for the health of millions, and for the health of the planet. His initiative started a movement that made an immeasurable difference, and it all started because he felt he could and ought to do something about it.

Leadership is about recognizing our own abilities to instigate positive change on whatever scale and in whatever context.

That being said, we often feel a sense of responsibility to do something to help the challenges we face in the world today. However, there is so much going on that needs our attention, we cannot possibly exercise leadership to deal with all the challenges in the world, no matter how much we may want to. In such situations, we should not let our sense of responsibility make us feel stressed or guilty. Instead, we should encourage and support those who are taking initiative to resolve the issues that we cannot attend to personally.

For instance, if we are focused on cleaning the oceans, we cannot exercise leadership to stop deforestation in the Amazon at the same time. However, we can maintain our focus and effort on our leadership initiative (cleaning the oceans), while offering whatever help we can to those who are working to end deforestation.

ACTION TIP:

Don't let yourself walk away from a leadership challenge because it's not your problem. If there is a problem and you care, make it your problem and take responsibility for fixing it as far as you are able to. Only by looking out for each other can we improve the world.

LEADERSHIP MANTRA

I care too much about the well-being of others to be passive.

LEADERSHIP DEMANDS HUMILITY

With experimentation and improvisation being major parts of leadership's repertoire, temporary failure is inevitable. We may fall down the ladder a few times before we can make our way to the top, and we must be prepared to accept our shortcomings.

Why is this important? As well as recognizing our own weaknesses, we need to be willing to ask others for help when dealing with issues and challenges. This is a vital part of leadership.

It can be difficult to ask others for help, and it may be even more difficult to accept this help, especially if people usually look to us for solutions. This is where humility plays a role. When we are humble, we will avoid personalizing the initiative and claiming it as our own. This means that we will be more willing to seek out help and discuss possible solutions with our supporters and allies. More importantly, we will be more likely to ask our opponents for help. They can provide an invaluable wealth of information about problems with the initiative.

Humility is fundamental because arrogance, overconfidence, pretentiousness, etc., are recipes for disaster that a so-called "leader" or the entire system will suffer from. Humility will provide a gentle reminder that we don't have all the answers, and that asking for help is important. After all, leadership is not personal, but is exercised for the sake of benefiting the system and its constituents.

When the late Nelson Mandela became president post-apartheid, he told the then chief of presidential protocol, John Reinders, that he was not well-experienced in the administrative duties of the presidency office. He proceeded to ask for his help, and the help of other experienced people.[21] This goes to show his dedication to his people and his country.

Reflection

Often in our lives, we have individuals who we associate with specific qualities or actions. Take a moment to think about anyone you know who is humble.

Now think about how this person (or these people) mobilized others and created beneficial change, no matter how small. Did they exhibit humility in their actions?

ACTION TIP:

Whenever you achieve something (whether your overall goal or a milestone along the way), actively seek humility. Remember that you are serving others, and do not be tempted by the glory of leadership. Stay humble even in your proudest moments.

LEADERSHIP MANTRA

Ego kills. Humility elevates. This is a collective effort. We are all heroes.

For your notes:

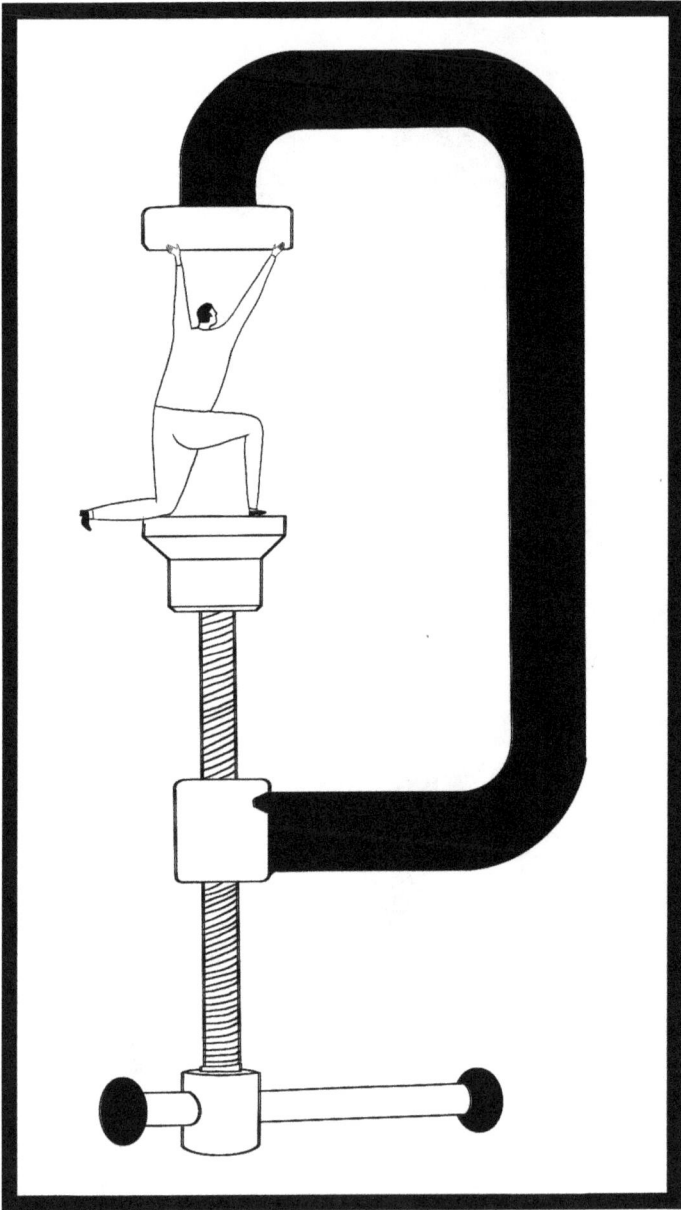

LEADERSHIP IS STRESSFUL

It would be nice to suggest that we could exercise leadership without experiencing stress; unfortunately, this is rarely the case in reality. If we want to live a life of minimal stress, we should think twice before exercising leadership. The unpredictability, the constant need to adapt to changes, the inherent responsibility we hold, and the resistance we may face are just some of the reasons that leadership is stressful, and often exceptionally so.

Sometimes even dealing with predictable machines and a regular routine can be stressful, so imagine mobilizing complex and unpredictable human beings to abandon their dysfunctional behaviors, beliefs, and attitudes, or deal with a dramatic change in their lives, and undertake a difficult journey of transformation.

Stress is one of the reasons many people shrink from exercising leadership. You may have heard people who gave up saying that they "could not handle the stress." The strength of a "leader" comes from their ability to accept and deal with the stressful environment, and to know how to maintain their physical, mental, and emotional sanity in the process.

ACTION TIP:

Recognize stress and actively seek ways to manage it. Set aside time for yourself, and do something that makes you feel relaxed. This could be as simple as deep breathing, or a sport, spending time in nature, meditation, reading, watching comedies, being with family and friends, praying, etc. Do not neglect yourself. Make time to unwind, even when life seems hectic. It will help you stay energized and allow you to power through difficulties.

LEADERSHIP MANTRA

I often need to step back to collect myself and recharge.

Leadership gives meaning to our lives:

There is no deeper source of meaning than to touch people's hearts and make a difference in their lives.

LEADERSHIP REQUIRES COURAGE

Many people who introduced phenomenal acts of leadership were, at the time, dubbed dreamers and ridiculed for even proposing their ideas. Those who courageously endured despite the negativity are the people whose actions we hear about today.

Leadership demands that we have the courage to actualize dreams and potentials. Leadership initiatives often strive to create a reality that initially seems unlikely or impossible, seeking to right fundamental wrongs in people, organizations, and societies. We will have to tap into our own self-confidence and be courageous enough to endure dismissive remarks and actions. We must trust ourselves and venture into the unknown, imagining "crazy" possibilities, and reaching for the stars. As Steve Jobs once said,

> "The people who are crazy enough to think they can change the world are the ones who do."

If we don't have enough inner strength and courage, we may give up when people mock us for our aspirations, abandoning the initiatives and allowing others to dictate reality. However, if we have enough courage, we will push past negativity and disbelief, and create something wonderful.

Remember that most major positive leaps in history, science, engineering, etc., were initially considered foolish, unrealistic, fictitious, or insane. The people who followed through with their thoughts and ideas are the ones who have shaped the course of history.

Reflection

Take a moment to look at your own life, or think about the stories you have heard, and recall those who dared to take the mantle of leadership and courageously introduce constructive change.

- How were they courageous?
- Did they experience resistance? How did they overcome ridicule and opposition?
- What can you, or those close to you, learn from the leadership acts of this person or group?
- If you were the one who exercised leadership, how did you show courage in the face of resistance?

ACTION TIP:

Use internal and external motivators to bolster your courage. Your purpose will be one of the most powerful motivators, because it is the reason for the whole initiative; return to it when you feel doubt or fear. Remember to stay close to people who raise your spirits and give you self-confidence.

LEADERSHIP MANTRA

I'm brave enough to face up to the challenges and promote growth.

LEADERSHIP INVOLVES SACRIFICE

There may be times when leadership seems glamorous. There may be moments when it appears to involve luxury, pleasure, fame, and so on. In some cases, exercising leadership from a position of authority, formally or informally, may mean these "benefits" apply, but only briefly. Acts of true leadership usually require sacrifices from people who are leading and from those being led. These could be emotional, physical, psychological, financial, professional, or relational. The first thing sacrificed by people who exercise leadership is emotional comfort, because they accept leadership's associated stress.

Unfortunately, many people who have led change have been overlooked, misunderstood, fired, mocked, humiliated, betrayed, persecuted, imprisoned, or even assassinated. In some cases, their families and loved ones have paid the price. I am sure if you look at the history of your own country or family, you will find plenty of examples of this reality.

The sacrifices depend on the context and scale of the change, with more significant changes requiring greater sacrifices. That is why true leadership can at times be immensely difficult. Some people may be unwilling to sacrifice for the sake of loved ones, let alone for the sake of strangers. If we want to exercise leadership, we must be prepared to give up our peace of mind, if need be, so that others can enjoy theirs.

Sacrifice is not only made by the person exercising leadership. When we empower individuals to embrace change and lead themselves towards a better reality, we are asking them to give up their comfort zones and a precious part of themselves, and experience stress, pain, loss, and inconvenience. This, disregarding any further forfeits they will make on the journey, is a sacrifice in itself. **Sacrifices are the price we pay today to create a better tomorrow. There is no escaping sacrifice if a significant and worthwhile reality is to be constructed.**

Despite the sacrifices acts of leadership will demand, there is nothing more rewarding and fulfilling than realizing that we are responsible for reducing people's pains, for putting a smile on their faces, for igniting hope in their eyes, and for adding joy to their lives. When we exercise leadership, we have the chance to give others a few extra moments of peace and reassurance throughout the journey. If we succeed, we will know that we played a part in making their lives more dignified.

There are many kinds of successes – financial, physical, emotional, professional – but nothing surpasses the feeling we experience when someone says, "thank you," or gives us a hug in which we can really feel their gratitude for our work.

Reflection

Reflect on your own life and the stories you have heard. As you reflect, remember that leadership is often arduous, and some sacrifices are too great for people to willingly endure them.

1. Consider a time when you made sacrifices for another person's benefit. Recall instances where people thanked you for having a positive impact on their lives.

2. Now recall a time when somebody else, even a stranger,

made a sacrifice, no matter how small, that impacted your life. Recall instances when you thanked others for elevating your life.

3. Think about a time when you made sacrifices to improve your own life.

4. Think of two people you have heard of that endured difficult times and willingly sacrificed aspects of their lives to help elevate the realities of others. How can their sacrifices be considered acts of leadership?

ACTION TIP:

Be prepared to make personal and non-personal sacrifices, but draw clear boundaries about what should not be sacrificed for the initiative. Doing this in advance will ensure you don't end up losing something important along the way.

Make sure to also embrace the deep gratification of the positive differences your sacrifices are making in other people's lives.

LEADERSHIP MANTRA

The future we're seeking is worth the sacrifices we will make.

LEADERSHIP WILL INVOLVE DISAPPOINTMENTS

There will be moments of celebration, but there will also be moments of disappointment. These will come from many different places. We may be disappointed in people around us, who will fail to deliver on their promises, or to support our work and initiatives. Sometimes the people closest to us – whether they support or oppose our initiatives – will misunderstand us. We may be disappointed in authority for not backing us, and in people unrelated to the initiative for not understanding the necessity of the changes we are proposing. We may even be betrayed by people we trust.

We may be disappointed in ourselves when we make miscalculations, or we fail to account for an opportunity. We may even feel disappointed in ourselves for struggling with the challenges of leadership, for contemplating abandoning our initiatives. Sometimes we will feel vulnerable, or give into temptations, or feel too tired to mobilize others. Sometimes the circumstances will suddenly change, or the very foundation of our plans will be disrupted.

Sometimes people will misinterpret the good that we are trying to do, especially those who will lose out if our initiatives succeed. They might interpret our actions as serving personal agendas; this is

195

often the case with great acts of leadership.

Throughout history, many social reformers were misunderstood when they challenged the ruling establishments. Their actions were misinterpreted as attempts to gain power and replace the existing establishment. They were not seen as people exercising leadership to try to help others.

Martin Luther, who is often associated with the Protestant Reformation, was a priest and theology scholar who protested against the Church's sixteenth century practice of absolving people of their sins in return for money. He published his 95 theses, which the Church saw as an attack to their authority. In response, he experienced resistance; his work was burned, and he was excommunicated. Despite this, when a rebellion began to pick up in response to his theses, he refused to support it.[22]

The reality is that we may be misunderstood, and it will disappoint us. We are trying to help people, and some of them will make our lives harder. It is important that we understand this fact. Remember, not everyone will be in our corner, and they will resist us because they don't understand what we are trying to do and why.

However, we might be the source of disappointment for others as well. Some people may invest their hopes in our initiatives, promises, and plans, and they go along with us because they trust us. When things don't work out the way we expect them to, we will experience the pain of feeling that we have let others down, that we have disappointed those who believed in the hopes that we gave them. That being said, we shouldn't be too hard on ourselves: this is just part of the journey.

ACTION TIP:

Return to this point whenever you suffer a setback, and remind yourself that leadership is often a journey of disappointments and failures, but persistence will help you realize your purpose.

Surround yourself with people who will support you when you are feeling drained or discouraged. It may also help you to make a list of great leaders and the setbacks they suffered; this will give you a sense of the "bigger picture," and will remind you that setbacks are not fatal.

LEADERSHIP MANTRA

We will have moments of disappointment, but we will eventually succeed.

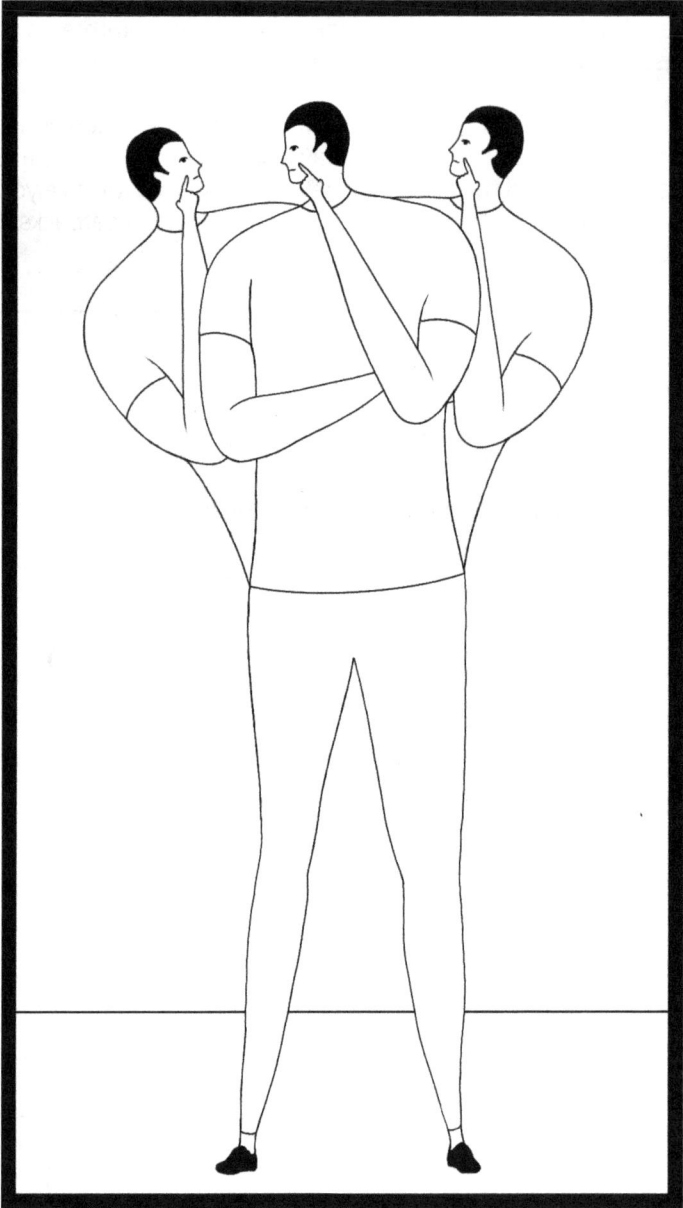

LEADERSHIP MAY INVOLVE MOMENTS OF SELF-DOUBT

One of the highlights of my life was meeting Nelson Mandela when he came to speak at the American University of Sharjah in the United Arab Emirates. Mandela told me a story about his first encounter with the warden in Robben Island prison.

As part of a prison ritual, the warden would come and aggressively lecture the prisoners in an attempt to establish his authority.

Mandela said that when the warden was giving his speech to the prisoners, who were standing side-by-side in a row, he would raise his voice, and stand very close to them, trying to intimidate them with his proximity and volume. Mandela told me something along these lines:

> **"As the warden went through his routine, when he approached me, I looked him in the eye and said, 'If you ever do anything you have just said, if you cross the line with me and my fellows, I will, as a lawyer, make your life very difficult."**

The warden was shocked at Mandela's words: "his face turned red like a tomato, but I was praying that he would not look at my knees, which were shaking as I spoke."[23]

Exercising leadership is often a tug of war between the person exercising leadership and the forces of resistance, which range from passive to extremely active, even malevolent. The pressure and stress of resistance will definitely induce moments of self-doubt. We will consider time and again whether the heavy costs of leadership are justified, whether we have made the right decisions, chosen the right approaches, or made major mistakes. We may question our own intelligence, and whether the rewards justify the costs.

We need to accept that we will not always have things under control, and this will cause those doubts to surface. Of course, we should give our doubts fair consideration because they might hold merit, but we shouldn't let them overwhelm us. We must accept that people suffer from doubts, and remember that our opponents may seek to exploit them.

ACTION TIP:

Recognize that you will suffer from doubts in advance so that you are prepared to deal with them. Write down your purpose and return to it when you need to counter your concerns. Log successes so you can see evidence of progress. Talk to friends, listen to other perspectives on your initiative, and surround yourself with people who keep your spirits high.

LEADERSHIP MANTRA

There will be moments of self-doubt. It's alright to be uncertain sometimes, but I won't let that stop me.

For your notes:

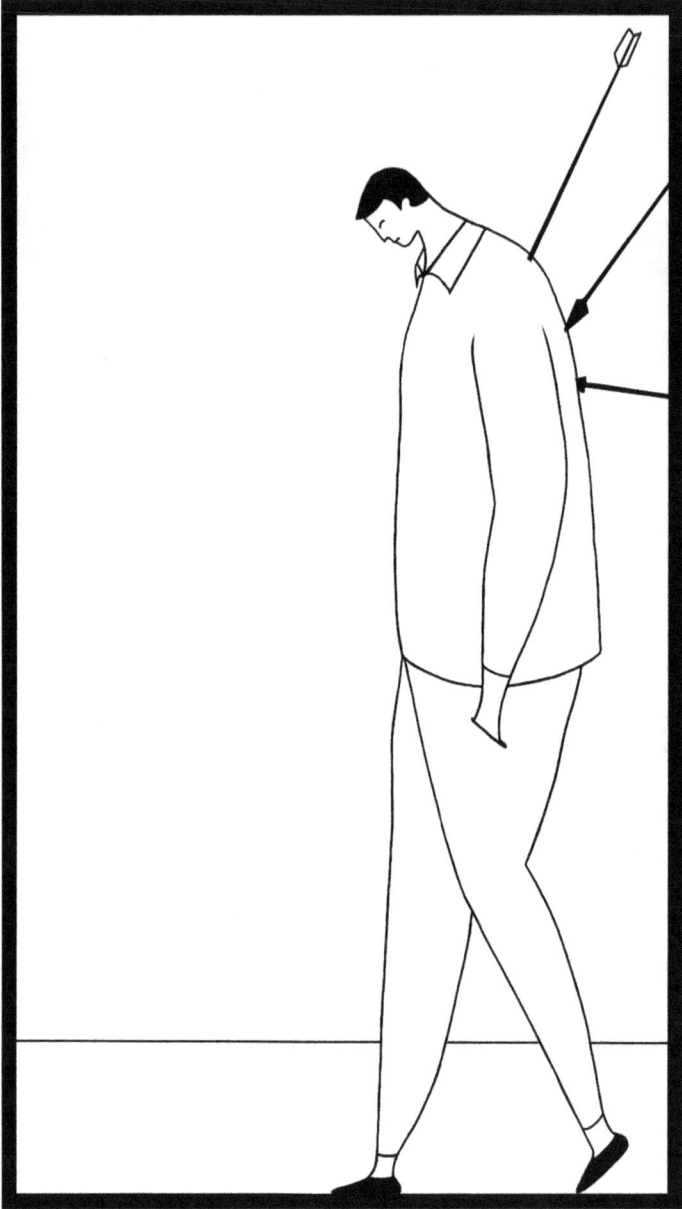

LEADERSHIP INCLUDES FEAR, BETRAYALS, TOLERATING PAIN, AND ENDURING INJUSTICE

Different people, as they are being mobilized to change, will react in different ways. The greater the sacrifice the initiative asks of them, the more intense their resistance will be. This will expose us to pain and fear. Some opponents may be aggressive and malicious; in some cases, our closest supporters and allies may "betray" us. We should recognize and prepare for these risks, and acknowledge to ourselves that we are likely to suffer if we try and exercise leadership.

In some cases, the system may be unjust and for the sake of creating a better reality, we will have to endure injustice. In fact, it might be this injustice that triggers a need for change. For an example, consider Branch Rickey and Jackie Robinson. The former was at the time (1945) the president of a major league baseball team (Brooklyn Dodgers) and the latter was the African American player who challenged the color barrier in the MLB (Major League Baseball). Branch Rickey decided that change needed to happen, and he believed that Jackie Robinson was the perfect person to help him end racial segregation in baseball.

Jackie Robinson tolerated racial slurs, hurled projectiles, fouls, and protests from his teammates. Some of his teammates refused to play with him or even share the locker-room. However, he stood his ground, took the hits, and played the game brilliantly, winning many accolades, including a World Series (the most important game in Major League Baseball).

Both Jackie Robinson and Branch Rickey made decisions that changed racial segregation in sports. Jackie Robinson said, "I knew I was kind of an experiment. The whole thing was bigger than me."[24]

Despite all the betrayals we might face, remember that acts of leadership often succeed even when it seems like there is no hope.

There will be people who will stab us in the back, but there will also be people who will surprise us in their loyalty. There will be supporters who will sacrifice to keep us in the game. They will inspire us with their commitment and willingness to follow the difficult path towards progress. They will encourage us to keep moving forward despite all the mess and obstacles.

Few successful leadership acts can be attributed solely to the resilience of the person exercising leadership. They are successful because of a solid circle of loved ones, friends, allies, and supporters, who provided hope and encouragement when the days seemed dark.

ACTION TIP:

Remind yourself that all these feelings are part of the package of leadership, and that even the greatest leaders and prophets experienced these problems. Stay focused on your purpose, and take care of yourself physically, spiritually, and emotionally. Accept the negative feelings which may come as a result of these obstacles, but do not let them consume you; you need to push through and move forward. Talk to others whenever you need support and encouragement.

LEADERSHIP MANTRA

Leadership can be tough, and life can be often unfair. There will be painful and frightening moments, but the chance of a better future is worth it.

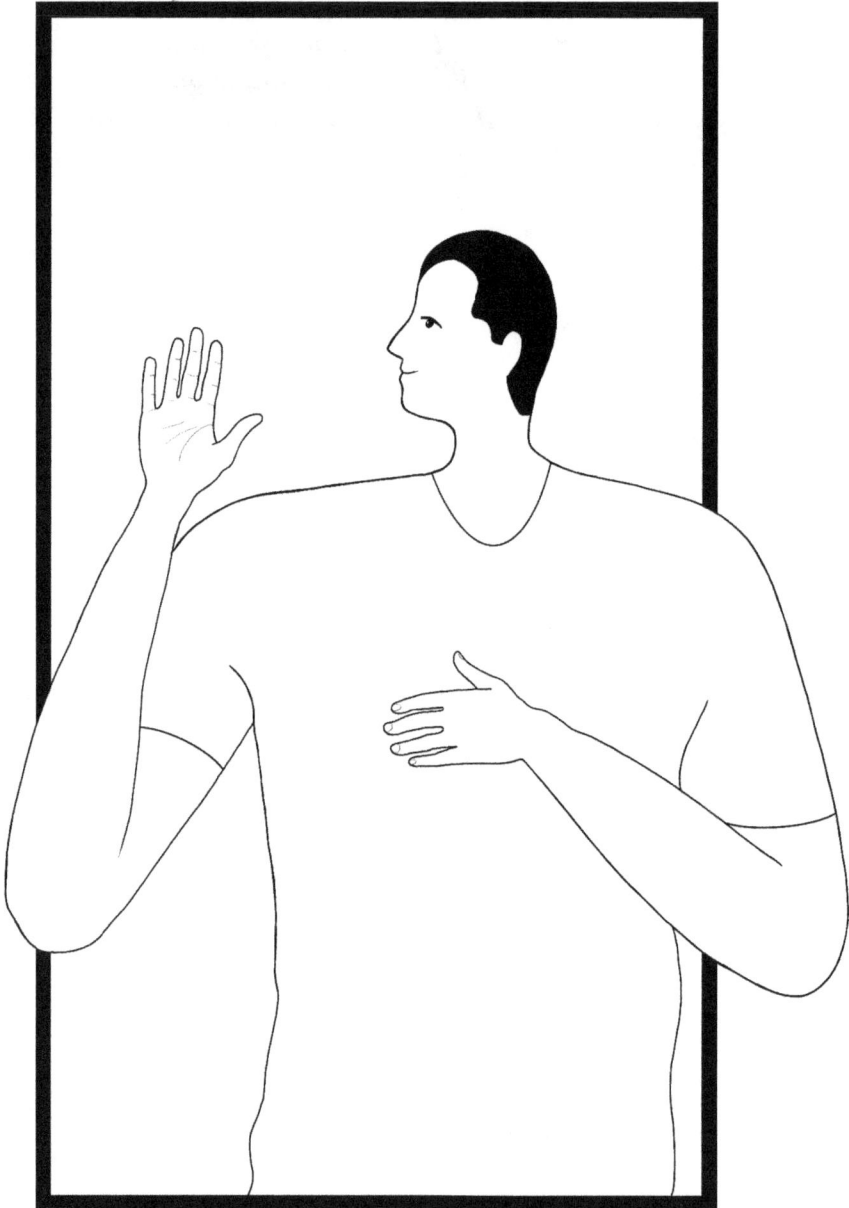

LEADERSHIP DEMANDS TRUST

Trust is the foundation of a functioning relationship. This is especially true when we are mobilizing people to abandon their comfort zones in the hope of gaining something better. People cannot be inspired by those they cannot trust. We will often need to earn people's trust before they will embrace the changes we are proposing.

Therefore, when we exercise leadership, our actions should work towards creating trust between ourselves and the system. If we are serious about helping others, our actions and words should reflect our genuine concern. Always bear in mind that everything we do and say should encourage the system to trust us.

It is equally important to ensure that everything which could damage this trust is avoided. For instance, even if we know bending the truth a little may inspire individuals, we should avoid the temptation. If we are caught in a lie, the trust we have built will be destroyed, and it will seem as though we have our own hidden agendas. Let us keep this saying in mind:

It takes a long time to build trust, it takes a short time to lose it, it takes an extremely long time to reconstruct it, and in some cases, it cannot be reconstructed.

Exercising leadership involves building trust through integrity, honesty, consistency, commitment, credibility, and a combination of other virtues. If we are exercising true leadership, these virtues will be almost second nature in our interactions.

ACTION TIP:

Make sure that you are clear about your intentions, and authentic when you speak or act. If you make a promise, deliver. If you cannot do something, say so as early as possible. Authenticity, predictability, credibility, and truth are key to building and maintaining trust.

LEADERSHIP MANTRA

My biggest asset is people's trust in me; I cannot afford to lose it.

Leadership should be about helping others,

Because we can and because it builds a better and more prosperous world for everyone.

LEADERSHIP AIMS TOWARDS THE SUSTAINABLE

We live in a closed system – Earth – and we are in one way or another connected across the globe. When we consider survival and growth, we cannot but be inclusive of our fellow Earth-dwellers. People, organizations, societies, and countries cannot continue to survive and grow at the expense of other people or life forms. This may work for a short while, and it may give us the illusion that what we are doing is to the benefit of our survival and growth. However, the truth is that what does not enhance and benefit life is usually not sustainable.

We are all living on the same planet, breathing the same oxygen, drinking the same water, and feeding off the same soil.

Consider this on a smaller scale. Take, for example, an exploitative government that does not look after its citizens, but siphons money out of the system and into the pockets of its officials. This government may make money at the cost of its people, but it cannot be sustainable; the people will either fail to survive, or they will overthrow the government. This compromises the government's long-term survival.

When a minority in a system attempts to thrive at the expense of others, this will in the long-term bring about resistance, which will intensify until something changes. Therefore, although in the short-term things may seem under control, surviving at the expense of others will ultimately lead to a degraded reality.

Let us consider a more current global concern. Human beings have been abusing nature and its atmosphere, animals, and terrain for many years, and at a rapidly increasing rate. As a result, environmental issues have become urgent. Short-term economic growth at the expense of other life forms and the ecosystem is making the situation critical. We only need to look at the exponential rise of greenhouse gases in the last century, or the increased extinction of species due to poaching, habitat loss, urbanization, and deforestation, to realize the magnitude of the problem.

Consider the recent increase in natural disasters (flooding due to deforestation, hurricanes due to unnatural temperatures, etc.) that we are experiencing. There is no doubt that our short-term mindset is affecting our lives, other organisms' lives, and the system overall. The survival of many species, including humans, could be compromised if this exploitative mindset does not change.

In conclusion, for the mobilization of individuals, organizations, and groups to be considered an act of leadership, it must be inclusive and consider the long-term implications. If it fails to do this, the mobilization will disregard the core purpose of leadership, which is the survival and growth of the system and its entire supporting ecosystem.

ACTION TIP:

Establish methods for checking your initiative is sustainable. Make sure you are not using up finite resources, or undermining a group of people. If you find something is going awry, you will need to do a full analysis to pinpoint what is wrong, and then look for ways to fix it. Do this regularly to make sure your initiative is not causing harm to the system.

LEADERSHIP MANTRA

I am aiming to create something which gives back what it takes. I want us to live in dignity, abundance and joy.

PART

3

WHAT
LEADERSHIP IS NOT

WHAT LEADERSHIP IS NOT

We have spent some time sifting through the soil to get to the roots of leadership. We have seen the origins of leadership, understood its necessity, looked at its components, and at its core purpose (i.e. survival and growth). We have also gone through some of the concepts that are part of the leadership discipline. All of this has helped us understand the spirit of leadership. The picture is almost complete, but we still need to remove some of the clutter and some confusing misconceptions.

This will allow us to see leadership more holistically as we clarify why these misconceptions are not "leadership."

Part of the confusion surrounding this subject is that leadership seems to have become synonymous with many different terms, subjects, and topics. A simple search for synonyms of leadership will get we words like management, authority, command, and administration.[1]

It's true that elements of the definition of leadership do apply to people in management positions or authority roles. You may be able to think of several historical examples of an authority figure who exercised true leadership. However, does this mean we need to be authority figures, managers, or people in positions of power to exercise leadership? Or that we must be charismatic, experts, or have followers to exercise leadership?

The answer is no. I know some of you will disagree, on at least one point, but I ask that you read on as we go through the reasons why some points are misconceptions of leadership. We will go through each point and start separating leadership from the other related, but not synonymous terms.

It is time to declutter the misconceptions and kick confusion out of the door, so that we can exercise leadership and create a dignified and fulfilling life for ourselves and those around us.

Leadership is not just about YOU*...

It is about ALL OF US.

* This does not refer to self-leadership

LEADERSHIP IS NOT AUTHORITY

Remember, authority and leadership are **two different, but equally important, disciplines.** *Authority* takes the form of a contract with a person or entity, where the person or entity is given power and resources on the condition that they carry out certain tasks. These tasks can usually be summarized in three points: Direction, Protection, and Order.[2] Let us take a moment to go over what these three points mean:

- **Direction** could include providing food, water, shelter, and the basic survival needs; or having a strategy or plan for growing a business; or creating job opportunities (for governmental authorities). Authority offers direction when it provides for the system and takes it down a sustainable path.

- **Protection** means shielding those under the responsibility of authority from external threats. These might be: enemy countries, competing companies engaging in corporate espionage, or external threats to a family or tribe. Authority is tasked with protecting the system from external forces that might threaten the survival and growth of the system.

- **Order** means creating and maintaining internal harmony. For example, parents are expected to create and maintain order at home, bosses in the workplace, school principals in their respective schools, and heads of state or governments in their respective countries. Order is achieved when rules and procedures are set and clearly communicated; when the mechanism for resolving internal conflict is established; and when the unwritten protocols are respected.

Authority exists in all contexts and can take on many forms. A school principal, a security counselor in the UN, a parent, a boss, God (for many) – all these forms constitute only one side of authority: the formal side. In this case, the authority figure holds a specific position within a hierarchy.

In general, formal authorities are granted their power and resources by those they are responsible for. These are the people or entities that "sign" the contract with their constituents, and they are expected to do their duties and provide the three services mentioned above.

What about the other side of authority? There are times when an individual who does not hold any formal position in the hierarchy may actually be running the show and calling all the shots. An informal authority is a person or entity that takes the reins, usually temporarily or behind the scenes, and informally fulfills the duties of formal authority. In short, they also take care of Direction, Protection, and Order. For example:

- A member of the family takes care of the children and provides direction, protection, and order when the parents are not there, or are unable to fulfill these duties.

- A president currently occupies the position of head of state, but his/her adviser is pulling the strings and "ruling" the country.

When we talk about authority and their duties, the core expectation is to create and maintain stability, sustainability, certainty, etc.

In such a state, people can live with the typical amount of stress that exists when people live together in groups. They expect authority to create an environment where they do not have to worry about issues that may disturb, or sometimes threaten, their lives.

What happens if authority fails to deliver? When authority does not uphold their end of the agreement, the people who are responsible for granting authority its power will work to take it away. It is within their rights to strip away the authority, or choose not to renew the contract, if authority is not delivering the required "services." For instance:

- A president is impeached, or is not reelected.
- An abusive parent is reported, imprisoned, stripped of their parental guardianship, or kicked out of the house.
- A CEO or manager is fired or given the choice to resign.
- A dictator is forced to step down in response to civilian revolutions and protests.

In the end, whatever the context, authority is about maintaining the status quo and harmony of the system (e.g. family, country, workplace), and they are given power to create stability within the system. If authority upsets the balance, they are subject to scrutiny, and at times they may be asked or forced to give up their position.

Leadership, on the other hand, is about changing things for the better, whether because of contextual pressure or to realize a better future – and it often means purposefully, strategically, and temporarily destabilizing the system and tipping the balance. It is about mobilizing individuals, societies, and countries to step away from their state of stability, predictability, and certainty, in the hope of creating a better reality or accepting a dramatic change.

Leadership could also mean transforming dysfunctional chaos, conflict, instability, and disequilibrium into a state of order, stability, and equilibrium.

Leadership might seek to:

- Solve a deeply entrenched problem (e.g. governmental corruption).

- Overcome a major threat (e.g. criminal syndicate).

- Change a collective, inappropriate mindset (e.g. racial and gender prejudices).

- Change behaviors (e.g. persuade people to decrease their carbon footprint).

- Find where an organization or team is stuck (e.g. experiencing a continuous crisis-management mode; internal conflicts; slow decision-making; waste of resources; inefficiency; failure to adapt to changing technologies and markets)

- Adopt new values (e.g. truth, responsibility, professionalism, honesty)

- Adopt new habits (e.g. eco-friendly practices; global collaboration).

Is it possible for authority figures to exercise leadership? Yes, it is possible. However, leadership is not conditional on authority, because as we established earlier, one could exercise leadership without holding a position of power – either directly or indirectly. For example, Malala Yousafzai was a girl when she was targeted and shot for speaking up against the Taliban and advocating for girls' rights to an education[3]; she still holds no formal authority, but continues to lead movements for gender equality.

Authority is focused on ensuring stability, while leadership is about creating strategic and purposeful instability. Authority is expected to maintain the status quo, while leadership is striving to bring about change and positive transformation. Authority breeds predictable results, while leadership asks people to take a leap of faith into the unpredictable. They may be related concepts, and ideally they should both serve the same purpose of survival and growth. However, they are totally different roles, and sometimes they play on almost opposing fields.

Given the hype surrounding the discipline of leadership, you may ask if one is better than the other, but remember that in our journey of survival and growth, we need both disciplines. We are not always experiencing upheaval, and although it is inevitable, change should never be introduced just for the sake of change. It is costly and should always be purposeful. When everything is working out beautifully, with a promising future, there is no reason to rock the boat. In this context, stability and certainty should be the system's aim. As Thomas Bertram Lance once said:

"If it ain't broke, don't fix it."

In short, our survival and growth, in a challenging world, require that we keep one foot in order, to ensure stability, and one foot in chaos, to create more potential.

Which discipline is required depends on what the context and general atmosphere call for. In the end, whatever serves the system's survival and growth should be at the forefront.

ACTION TIP:

Before you begin an initiative, study the situation carefully, and decide whether you are attempting to maintain the status quo, or make major changes. If it's the former, bear in mind that you are not leading, but exercising authority. Make sure you're clear about this.

LEADERSHIP MANTRA

I don't need to be the boss to lead.

LEADERSHIP IS NOT MANAGEMENT

What about management? Surely leadership needs management? Possibly, but there are marked differences between the two.

Management is more closely related to authority than it is to leadership. Authority is to management as electricity is to a motorized machine. The machine cannot operate without electricity, and management cannot function without authority.

For instance, a president cannot manage his/her presidential duties without the authority the position grants him/her; and a CEO that doesn't have any authority cannot fulfill his/her "executive" duties. Management cannot instill order and create harmony if it does not have authority.

Just imagine a manager in an organization trying to manage the organization's operations by setting priorities, allocating resources, designing plans of action, enforcing control mechanisms, spending money, and hiring and firing staff without having the authority to do so. To manage, one needs to have some control and power over their team, group, or organization.

Without authority, a person in management cannot[4]:

- **Plan.** A person needs access to resources and information so that they can formulate different plans.

- **Organize.** A person must have control over the system to ensure that everything is in its right place for a plan to be carried out.

- **Manage Staff.** A person must have some control over who joins and leaves the team and who is responsible for each task. They must also have the power to hold people accountable for their actions, rewarding those who do their jobs and punishing those who don't.

- **Control.** A person cannot manage without control, and they will find it difficult to enforce guidelines and policies without the control that their position offers them.

Management is about using one's authority to ensure that a complex system, made up of multiple interdependent components, works harmoniously to fulfill a defined purpose. It is about using the resources and power at one's disposal in the most efficient and productive way. On the other hand, leadership is about transformation, and mobilizing people to seek a more optimal state of being.

While leadership can make use of the tools afforded to management for the sake of mobilization and transformation, it does not need these tools to achieve its goal. History shows that sometimes authors, musicians, artists, social volunteers, and even spiritual figures managed to mobilize thousands without access to the resources and power afforded to management. They did so solely through the "power" of inspiration, courage, persistence, resilience, meaning, truth, and responsibility.

Management and leadership are different acts that can be carried out within a group, organization, society, and/or country. Leadership is not conditional on management, just as it is not conditional on authority. However, a manager can exercise leadership, and the person exercising leadership can manage.

I recall a time in the 1970s and '80s when management and its related terms were all the rage, while leadership as a discipline was not widely acknowledged. Management was so trendy that universities even created special degrees solely for the purpose of teaching management. It reached a point where universities worldwide competed to create and promote management programs, trying to attract students with these "fashionable" degrees.

The tide has turned towards glorifying leadership and belittling management. There are an increasing number of studies, articles, and opinions that are skeptical about the importance of pursuing management degrees. Sometimes, management has negative connotations, and is criticized for promoting static thinking and a fixed mindset – as opposed to the growth mindset that is at the core of leadership.

Personally, I would suggest that both management and leadership are equally important disciplines that are necessary for the survival and growth of any social and organizational system.

There are times when change is necessary, and the system needs to be mobilized to evolve despite the associated instability and stress. After the change, social systems need to experience stability, certainty, and predictability, and management plays a role in making that a reality. Without good management, the system will be unable to root firmly in the enhanced reality.

Systems that understand the difference between leadership and management strive to create a better reality and then work to maintain it. Such systems know how to alternate intelligently between the two states: stability and change. In other words, they know when management is needed more than leadership, and when the time is right for leadership to take over.

ACTION TIP:

As with the previous section, carefully diagnose the situation before you act, and decide which discipline applies to what you want to do. Differentiating between authority, management, and leadership will prevent chaos along the way. If you are unclear, it's likely that everyone else will be as well, so think carefully about how your plans interact with the system, and whether you are promoting change or promoting stability.

LEADERSHIP MANTRA

I'm empowering people to grow, not managing their energies.

LEADERSHIP IS NOT ENTREPRENEURSHIP

Leadership and entrepreneurship share extensive common ground. Both require the individual to have enough courage to experiment with new ideas, and to question the status quo. They must actively seek solutions to problems they see, and then work to actualize the solutions.

They also share a high tolerance for failure. It is widely acknowledged that, on average, several entrepreneurs or their ideas fail before they succeed.[5] Leadership initiatives also carry a risk of failure, so persistence, courage, and other virtues are necessary. Both concepts require the individual to have faith in themselves, and to try again when faced with difficulties or failures, learning from mistakes and constantly seeking to improve.

Both disciplines also require the individual to be able to mobilize and enthuse others. This is particularly true for entrepreneurs during the high risk and uncertain stage of introducing a new business idea or start-up. Good communication skills and a vision of the future are crucial for entrepreneurs and people exercising leadership alike.

The lives of famous entrepreneurs, like Richard Branson and Elon Musk, are full of examples where acts of leadership took place. Their companies were not always successful – naturally, they experienced setbacks and disappointments – but in those moments, they exercised leadership to mobilize people through turbulent times.

So, you might ask: how are leadership and entrepreneurship different?

Leadership and entrepreneurship should not be used interchangeably. Not every entrepreneur can by default exercise leadership, which requires mobilizing people and groups through constructive change, evolution, and transformation. Often, entrepreneurs can be brilliantly successful in introducing projects and ideas in high-risk situations, but fail to take these into full maturity or make them scalable, to realize their full potential. This is mainly because entrepreneurs may lack the fundamental leadership skills that are required to mobilize people in complex organizations and systems.

ACTION TIP:

If you have a tolerance for high risks and find meaning in promoting new ideas, invest in building your leadership and entrepreneurial skills. Your success will often depend on applying both sets of skills. Always remember, whether in entrepreneurship or leadership, that the name of the game is taking a substantial risk that is justified by a worthwhile meaning.

LEADERSHIP MANTRA

The purpose of leadership is to mobilize others toward their progress. I seek to serve others, not just myself.

LEADERSHIP DOES NOT REQUIRE SUPERHUMAN ABILITIES

There are leadership books that discuss what a "leader" should look like, what qualities s/he should have, and how these characteristics help to make this person a "successful leader."

There is no doubt that it would be brilliant for a person exercising leadership to have all the traits and characteristics these books list. However, I find that this asks too much of the person wishing to exercise leadership, or any person really.

It is rare to find people who have all the characteristics on those long lists. They may embody some, or most of them, but even so, they will be weaker in some areas than others. To make so many traits prerequisites of leadership demands too much. It will discourage and dishearten anyone interested in the subject; they simply cannot meet these unrealistic requirements.

A study of the people who are widely regarded as "great leaders" shows that they are just normal human beings, like you and me. They have their strengths and weaknesses.

Some of those who exercised great leadership:

- Were extroverts (e.g. Margaret Thatcher)[6]
- Were introverts (e.g. Mahatma Gandhi)[7]
- Had a temper (e.g. John Adams)[8]
- Were optimistic (e.g. Dwight D. Eisenhower)[9]
- Suffered from depression (e.g. Abraham Lincoln)[10]

These people are famous for the changes which they initiated. However, remember that each did so within a specific context, and with both strengths and weaknesses. It may be that their strengths were exactly matched to their particular challenge, while their weaknesses offered minimal hindrance. If we were to put any of these leaders in front of a different challenge, they might not be so effective. The success of leaders is largely dependent on the situation.

Different leadership challenges call for different skills and attitudes. While a person might have some skills that could fit the requirement of leading in a certain situation, the same person might lack the relevant attributes that are required to lead in another situation.

For instance, Winston Churchill was considered a hero when he led his country in WWII[11]. The same Churchill resigned from the government years before WWII[12], when he was held responsible for a military blunder that cost more than 34,000 of his countrymen their lives, and injured almost 80,000 more – the battle of Gallipoli.[13] He then failed to be reelected as prime minister immediately after WWII because people did not believe that he could lead the economic reconstruction of his country.[14]

Leadership is not about having the full catalog of positive traits. It is primarily about building the capacity to deal with the challenges or opportunities we face. However, we should always try and improve our repertoire of strengths given the opportunity. Remember that a crucial part of leadership is growing and being willing to learn.

True leadership comes from using our strengths, whatever they may be, to deal with challenges or opportunities, and to mobilize others, create value, and realize an elevated reality. If we focus on traits and characteristics without understanding how effectively these qualities deal with situations, we may rush to call a person a "leader" when in fact they may not be able to rise to the occasion – not without building different capacities first.

Do not apply impossible standards to leadership. The "great leaders" in history made strides of progress, showed incredible resolve, and introduced significant change, but they also made mistakes, miscalculated, misjudged, and possibly aggravated situations before making the right moves.

You don't need to be superhuman to exercise leadership.

ACTION TIP:

Remember that you are only human – as was every other great leader throughout history. Everybody has weaknesses and flaws, and these will play out differently in different situations. What may hinder you in one scenario could help you in another.

Distrust fixed criteria for leadership, and remember to keep building on your current abilities. As long as you are prepared to learn and grow, and you seek improvement for yourself and others, you are ready to lead.

LEADERSHIP MANTRA

I will continue to learn and lead in spite of my imperfections.

LEADERSHIP IS NOT INFLUENCE

This one may come as a surprise, but leadership is not influence. Influence is a process and a technical tool. It can be utilized for a beneficial purpose, as well as for a harmful one. Sometimes "leaders" influence people to act in a way that comes at other's expense, or even at their own expense. They may ask them to make sacrifices that will do more harm than good. Occasionally, people are coerced and forced to follow a "cause" they do not support, and we sometimes rush to call such influencers "leaders."

If someone had a gun to a person's head, s/he would probably follow the gun-wielder's requests, but can this type of influence be called leadership? When the head of a gang influences the neighborhood youth to join the gang and partake in criminal activities, is this what we want to call leadership? Now think about less extreme examples of such influence, and consider whether any form of negative coercion is truly leadership.

Leadership is about mobilizing people, encouraging them to take control of their lives and embrace change because it represents a better future. Done well, an act of leadership can mobilize an entire nation to embrace transformational change. People's willingness to change because they are driven by purpose is crucial to exercising leadership.

Of course, leadership does need to influence people in order to mobilize them. However, it is arguable that leadership uses influence, rather than embodying influence. Therefore, when we talk about purpose-driven leadership, we are talking about conditional influence that is better termed mobilization for a good purpose that ensures people's well-being.

To say that leadership is about influence turns leadership into a technical capacity, and deprives it from the ethical and moral dimension that we want to reattach to leadership. The leadership that we want to define and exercise in the 21st century is value-based and seeks to create beneficial change. It is not just a technical skill, but it has a more important layer which is driven by truth, purpose, and meaning, creates value, and mobilizes towards fulfillment.

Finally, remember that, apart from self-leadership, leadership is always about helping people for their own sake – while influence may be entirely self-motivated, and may cause harm to others, including those being mobilized.

Reflection

Try to think of somebody you know or have heard of who wields great influence over others.

- What were their intentions?
- Can their acts be considered part of the leadership realm? If not, why? How were they misusing their influence?

ACTION TIP:

Do not pressure people excessively, or try to manipulate them into following you, even if you believe you are doing it for their benefit. To exercise leadership, you should aim to empower and inspire. If you find it difficult to determine whether you are overstepping the boundary, put yourself in the shoes of the person you are mobilizing. Decide whether you would feel "used" or pushed, and this will help you determine if your methods are excessive.

LEADERSHIP MANTRA

I will always avoid manipulating the people around me. The ends don't always justify the means.

LEADERSHIP IS NOT ABOUT HAVING FOLLOWERS

When we say leadership needs followers, we are implying that there are people who are leading, and moving in a certain direction, with others following them wherever they go. An image that comes to mind is that of a tour guide holding a colored flag as s/he moves around a museum or archaeological site, with a group of visitors following close behind. This scene suggests that there is a person who has the answers, knows the direction, and is dictating where the group goes – essentially, "follow me."

People who exercise leadership may have followers, but having followers does not necessarily determine whether a person is exercising leadership or not – it is not a required condition. Leadership mobilization is about focusing on **following an idea and purpose,** rather than on a **"follow me" mentality.**

There are numerous ways to exercise leadership, and many will not result in amassing followers. Some acts of leadership raise awareness and inspire others to take action. In a sense, they mobilize a person or group to act and create positive change. However, they only serve as the inspiration for other acts of leadership.

For instance, the novel "The Jungle" by Upton Sinclair increased awareness of issues with food hygiene in Chicago factories. This sparked a movement by an upset public, which brought this issue to the attention of US President Theodore Roosevelt. In that same year, Roosevelt signed a bill that led to the eventual formation of the Food and Drug Administration (FDA)[15]. Sinclair inspired change through his writing and helped people realize something needed to change to create a better reality – which is considered an act of leadership. Although he did gain acclaim later in his life, he did not really have "followers" as a result of his act of leadership. Instead, his book raised awareness and inspired others to exercise leadership and bring about significant change.

When we are exercising leadership sometimes we will have followers; in other cases we will not. Similar to Sinclair's case, some people have exercised leadership that mobilized and inspired others to take action; they didn't have followers. In other examples, including some of the ones mentioned in this book, people exercised leadership and they had followers. They mobilized others to follow their example, or they helped guide their followers down a specific path.

When people follow a person who is exercising leadership, they do so because the person is an embodiment of their fears, hopes, dreams, etc. S/he represents ideals, becoming the personification of an individual's concerns and aspirations. Therefore, people follow this person not because of who s/he is but because of the purpose the initiative is calling for; they follow the person who is representing a cause that resonates with them.

Consider celebrities in 2019 and earlier: many of them have millions of followers. When they make a fashion statement or a lifestyle change, often their followers will make the same changes. Does this mean that every change they make is an act of leadership? Not if the change is not purpose-driven and aimed at making a change for the better. For instance, when a celebrity changes their hairstyle, this fashion choice, which may be adopted by his/her followers, doesn't benefits people's survival and growth. However, some of their followers will make this change. The point is that we cannot say that having followers is necessary for exercising leadership. People can have followers without exercising leadership.

Leadership is about mobilizing people towards a life of meaning and purpose, rather than to follow a person. The loyalty and commitment of the people should be evoked to follow the cause of creating good, rather than the person who is leading.

As long as an initiative has a purpose, inspires people to mobilize and create beneficial change, and ensures the survival and growth of the system and its constituents, it will be considered an act of leadership – with or without personal followers.

ACTION TIP:

Resist measuring your success by its followers – or its opponents. These may come and go. Do not be discouraged if nobody will stand behind you. As long as you know your initiative is for the good of the system and its constituents, you can be sure that it is an act of leadership.

LEADERSHIP MANTRA

If the path is right, I will walk it regardless of whether I walk alone.

LEADERSHIP DOES NOT NEED PERMISSION

Leadership needs permission." I don't subscribe to this idea. When we say that leadership needs permission, we are implying that one needs permission to inspire, mobilize, or do good. That is definitely not the case. Leadership often involves mobilizing people to make beneficial decisions and changes that they are unaware they can make, or even that they don't want to make. If a person had to wait for permission to inspire others, s/he would wait a lifetime!

The problem with this concept is that it confuses leadership with authority: authority is contingent on the permission of the people who have granted authority. Without permission, it cannot operate.

On the other hand, leadership may sometimes be a solo enterprise. Without asking for permission, many "leaders" knew what they had to do – what they thought was right – and did it. Those who were inspired to follow in their footsteps had to adhere to the rules that upheld the initiative's purpose. It was the beliefs and values of the leaders that drove their acts of leadership.

Gandhi did not ask for anyone's permission when he started his *Satyagraha movement* in South Africa. He didn't ask for permission to boycott British products, or to refuse to pay the salt tax the British introduced in India. He also didn't ask permission to conduct multiple fasts over his lifetime to protest injustice, unfairness, and violence, among other things[16]. Gandhi famously said: "First they ignore you, then they laugh at you, then they fight you, then you win." Those who were inspired by his campaign later joined him, adopting his values and principles, while those who did not accept his rule of nonviolence were rejected by him.

Alex Schulze and Andrew Cooper, who started a movement when they founded 4Ocean in 2017 to clean up plastic from the ocean, did not ask for permission. They just realized that there was a problem and started cleaning the oceans and beaches.[17] Those who were inspired by them asked their permission to join 4Ocean in accordance with its rules, principles, and values.

The concept of needing permission to exercise leadership is limiting, and it reduces hope in improving the condition of our planet. We don't need permission to exercise leadership because we don't need permission to do the right thing, to challenge, to try, to experiment with bold ideas, to disrupt, to initiate, and to inspire.

ACTION TIP:

If you see a problem that you can fix, fix it without waiting for somebody to tell you that you can. Great opportunities are missed when people wait for permission, so ensure you take action whenever you feel able to.

LEADERSHIP MANTRA

I don't need permission to do good and inspire others.

LEADERSHIP DOES NOT DEMAND CHARISMA

There is a popular misconception that to exercise leadership, a person needs charisma – charm. This can be a dangerous suggestion because it implies that the mobilized group has been "charmed" by the person exercising leadership.

If you are familiar with folklore and fairy tales, you will probably know that when someone is "charmed," they are usually in a semi-conscious, mesmerized state, willing to do anything the "charmer" asks of them. They lose their ability to think critically and make conscious, purposeful decisions.

This "charmed" state exists to a lesser degree in reality; there are people in the real world who play on people's fears and hopes, sometimes to the point that these individuals are in a semi-hypnotic state, willing to accept all that the "charmer" says as true, and to do as s/he asks of them.

Consider Jim Jones, who, almost 60 years ago, managed to create a cult of people who had fallen prey to his charms and promises of a utopian life. He not only convinced his followers to hand over all their possessions, but to relocate to a commune in Guyana called Jonestown. In 1978, he managed to convince more than nine hundred people to drink poison, resulting in mass suicide; it became known as the "Jonestown Massacre."[18]

Saying that leadership is contingent on charisma undermines the rationality of making necessary changes. People ought to be inspired by the act of leadership, rather than by the person exercising leadership. Remember that the person exercising leadership should not "own" their act, and therefore their charisma – or lack thereof – should not be a determining force in whether people choose to embrace the proposed change.

This is certainly not to say that a charismatic person cannot lead. If we manage to inspire others with our visions for the future, many people will see us as charismatic even if we are not notably so. Charisma is not inherently dangerous, but it is dangerous to assume that leadership is contingent on charisma.

Reflection

Think of the people you admire. Who would you say is charismatic?

- How have they used this charisma to help others?
- Have they ever taken advantage of others? How?

> **ACTION TIP:**
>
> Always work in reality, giving people reasons to follow your ideas, rather than trying to sway them with pretty words. You should present a likable front, but ensure people genuinely believe in your cause, rather than in your persona, if you want to lead and empower them.

LEADERSHIP MANTRA

I don't want people to follow me. I want them to follow the path to progress and prosperity.

LEADERSHIP IS NOT ABOUT HAVING A RIGID AND DOGMATIC MINDSET

The dictionary defines dogma as, "a principle or set of principles laid down by an authority as incontrovertibly true."[19]

When we exercise leadership, we need to have the flexibility to refine our thinking, to listen to others, and to check the accuracy of our interpretations of reality. If our thinking is unsound, we may make the wrong strategic choices, assuming that this is the right and only direction to take. Furthermore, if we misinterpret reality, we will have mobilized people to make a change, only to make a mess of the whole situation and make matters worse. The price we pay will vary, and sometimes it can have fatal consequences.

The purpose of leadership is to reduce suffering and pain, to add value and beauty to people's lives and the world, to elevate their lives, and to create an enhanced reality. This requires us to have an inclusive attitude and an open mind. Remember, leadership is not about us, so when people point out the blind spots in our interpretations, that should not bother us. It is not about how smart we are, or how we see things. Instead, we should engage our support networks, and sometimes even our opponents, to consider as many perspectives as we can to avoid blind spots and improve the chances of success.

Leadership is about following a purpose that is flexible, and does not come at the expense of others' freedoms, rights, and lives. A leadership initiative is fueled by a strong, inclusive, beneficial, meaningful, and inspirational purpose that takes a long-term perspective and focuses on creating progress, solving problems, spreading care, removing pain, enduring hardships, and embracing love.

ACTION TIP:

Remind yourself that it is a sign of intelligent behavior to be flexible and open-minded, to listen to others, and to enrich your thinking with different perspectives.

LEADERSHIP MANTRA

It is not about the way I see the future; it is about creating the best future for us all.

LEADERSHIP IS NOT JUST ABOUT HAVING A VISION

A vision by itself does not usually involve action, and exercising leadership requires mobilization. Leadership is about mobilizing people, organizations, and communities to realize a vision of a better reality, but having a vision alone does not automatically translate into exercising leadership.

Vision is a powerful tool of leadership. In the hands of purposeful leadership, vision can inspire, encourage, and energize others, providing them with hope, perseverance, resilience, energy and enthusiasm. It is like looking at a beautiful picture of how the future could be. This helps people *see* and *feel* the potential future, which encourages them to embark upon the sacrificial journey that will create that future. Having a vision of the possible reality can help to actualize that reality.

Some of the most effective visions are those that were constructed by the people who will be mobilized to realize it.

I was recently invited by the government of the Sultanate of Oman to deliver a speech at a major national conference about Oman's vision for the year 2040. The Sultanate of Oman has wisely involved its citizens in the creation of a shared vision for the twenty years to come. It was a collective effort, where tens of thousands of people took part in massive, nationwide discussions.[20]

This allowed the people to voice their hopes, aspirations, and fears. It was not a top-down vision imposed by the government, but was constructed bottom-up by the citizens, who actively participated in envisioning their aspired future. After this massive exercise, the government published a draft of the vision for the whole world to provide feedback on before deciding on the final version of the vision.

Vision can be a great tool for purposeful mobilization, but without an intelligent strategy and brilliant execution, visions are just dreams.

Acts of leadership are needed to turn a vision into a reality.

When times are tough, sometimes vision may only be about surviving threatening circumstances. Sometimes what we need most is the hope that one day things will get better. A vision of a happy ending can increase people's resilience in dealing with their hardships, allowing them to persevere in the face of setbacks, and to reconstruct their shattered realities.

In business, an inspiring vision can help a company survive the storms of a severe economic recession, until the markets pick up again.

We need to remember that although visions are useful, just having a vision doesn't constitute leadership. Anybody can construct a dream about their aspired future. The challenge is to mobilize people to realize this vision, and to ensure that the vision truly offers a version of reality that would be beneficial for the entire system, not just for the people who have the vision.

A vision must entail making life better for the group in a sustainable way. There are instances where a vision is a nightmare instead of a dream. The person perpetuating the vision may successfully mobilize others, but towards a negative outcome. Many cults, terrorist organizations, and racist or oppressive entities had "visionary leaders." Indeed, the vision often seems to be a selling point for many of their followers. However, these visions fail to promote the well-being of others, and therefore are discounted from the purpose-driven leadership that we should promote to ensure a better life for all on the planet.

A vision can easily be a manifestation of the insecurities, ambitions, and prejudices of the so-called "leaders." Power, influence, and/or charisma might be used to mobilize people to embrace this self-serving, egocentric, and sometimes grandiose vision. This is not only an abuse of power, but can be quite dangerous because it cannot possibly lead to a better reality if it is riddled with unethical values.

Let us consider one of the most infamous historical figures: Adolf Hitler. He definitely had a vision. However, we can all agree that a Nazi-occupied/-dominated Europe led by a brutal "supreme leader," against the will of the majority of its people[21], is not the mark of the leadership and vision that we should promote.

"Leadership is the capacity to translate vision into reality."

– Warren G. Bennis

ACTION TIP:

Your leadership act may stem from a vision of a better future, but don't allow this vision to usurp reality. Visions change, but purpose doesn't. Ensure you are flexible, adaptive, and realistic. Just as many great leaders have had to accept improvements over perfection (think of the "I have a dream" speech, which is still only a vision rather than a reality for many), be prepared to make compromises. Achieving something – even if it isn't the perfection you had hoped for – is better than achieving nothing because you were too rigid about how the future must look.

LEADERSHIP MANTRA

If the initiative brings about healthy growth, it has succeeded, regardless of what I visualized. I see us living in abundance, prosperity, and joy.

LEADERSHIP DOES NOT EQUATE TO BEING AN EXPERT

Some definitions suggest that exercising leadership means that we need to be more knowledgeable than those we are working to mobilize. For instance, a tour guide is expected to have more knowledge than the tourists – that is their job. However, as we have already mentioned, when it comes to the "follow me" mentality, we are talking more about authority than leadership.

Being an expert is usually a good thing; we are likely to have a better understanding of what the system needs if our initiatives fall within our fields of expertise. In addition to this, being experts can give us credibility with the people we wish to mobilize. They will be more inclined to trust our judgments if we have a strong understanding of our respective subjects. However, we will often find that we are leading in areas which we are not experts in – or at least in areas which have other more knowledgeable people. That doesn't mean we can't exercise leadership.

Leadership sometimes calls for improvisation and learning on the go. People throughout history have succeeded in bringing about significant changes without being experts in the area where they were

249

introducing change – many of these individuals are well known, and their examples are mentioned throughout this book.

Mahatma Mohandas K. Gandhi was a trained and certified lawyer, but he had not studied politics, governance, or public policy. He was neither an "expert" in mobilizing a nation, nor an "expert" in helping a country gain its independence. What he had was the belief that there was a better reality for him and his people. This was enough for him to reject his current reality and disobey the rules of the British authorities.[22]

Therefore, expertise can improve our chances of implementing successful leadership initiatives, but it is not essential for leadership.

ACTION TIP:

Don't shy away from doing something because you think other people have a greater understanding of the situation than you do. You can always learn more and continue to educate yourself in your leadership journey. In any case, nobody has perfect knowledge – learn as you go.

When it comes to leading, make sure you fulfill these basic requirements:

- Clarity of the purpose of your leadership intervention.
- The skill and capacity to mobilize people.

Other kinds of expertise are an advantage, but they can be acquired by involving other experts and increasing your understanding of the field later.

LEADERSHIP MANTRA

My role is to be an "expert" in mobilizing the experts.

BEING EFFECTIVE DOESN'T EQUATE TO EXERCISING LEADERSHIP

Not every effective act of mobilization is automatically regarded as an act of leadership. Sometimes, we will find that autocratic thinking can be effective; so too can democratic thinking. Stubbornness can be effective, as can flexibility. Ruthlessness can be effective, as can mercy. Bluntness can be effective, as can politeness.

The question that determines if an effective act constitutes an act of leadership is, "Why introduce this intervention?" We must consider what kind of impact this "effective leadership" is creating. Most of us can agree that a dictator may be effective, but ruling through fear and manipulation cannot be leadership – at least not leadership that aims to mobilize people towards better realities.

No matter how effective an act is, if it is not purpose-driven and value-driven, if it does not aim to enhance the human condition and eliminate unnecessary pain in the long run, then it doesn't fit into the leadership discipline that we should promote. In other words, if the core purpose of leadership is not fulfilled, then no matter how effective an initiative is, it cannot be counted among the true acts of leadership.

For example: in the late 1800s, Frederick Winslow Taylor transformed the way that companies operated, and increased the levels of productivity. He introduced a concept called *scientific management,* which observed how laborers were operating, and then looked for the "best way" for them to carry out their tasks. Through his method, he gave managers the power to dictate who did what, and how it should be done. This allowed any laborer, regardless of their skill level, to learn the optimal way to get their assigned job done.

Taylor also introduced a form of incentivized pay, where the worker would be compensated depending on how much they worked. This and other changes in the workplace increased efficiency but invariably decreased worker satisfaction and led to strikes and protests. Eventually, this system became so prevalent and the tasks so optimized and repetitive that workers were slowly replaced by machines, ushering in the phase of automation. Consequently, people lost their jobs and were no longer able to purchase the products they were originally working on. As such, demands decreased, and supplies skyrocketed.[23]

In the end, an effective initiative that had changed the face of industries led to a worse reality for some employees. Although Taylor's initiatives were highly effective, they did not lead to a higher quality of life for most people involved.

In another example, poultry farms in the United States often focus on being effective. Efficiency is so vital to the organizations that some employees are abused and denied their rights. Those who work on the line are not allowed to go to the bathroom before they complete their work, and given a specified time interval. People may be subject to punishment or dismissal if they stop the work to go to the bathroom. As a result, people have either limited their fluid intake, often becoming dehydrated, or they have urinated on themselves. Some have even resorted to wearing adult diapers so that they can relieve themselves and continue working.[24] This abuse is efficient but is definitely not an act of leadership by the employers of poultry farms.

On the other hand, there may be times when our initiatives do fit the requirements of leadership, but fail to be effective. This might be because the system isn't ready, or because of some other uncontrollable factors in the environment. Not being effective does not disqualify our interventions from being considered as acts of leadership.

ACTION TIP:

When considering your initiative, make a few sanity checks to decide whether it counts as leadership.

- Why are you introducing this initiative?
- What is the expected outcome? How does this initiative make things better?
- How does it consider the collective benefit to the system? Is it about getting things done regardless of the costs?
- Is it driven by love and care?

LEADERSHIP MANTRA

Being effective does not necessarily mean being right.

LEADERSHIP IS NOT POWER

Power can be religious, political, legal, physical, moral, martial, economic, etc.; either in a formal capacity or an informal one.

Formal power is an authority term. Leadership is about mobilizing with or without formal power.

Power is part of the technology of leadership and can be a wonderful tool if we have access to it. However, it is how we use power that determines whether we are exercising leadership, not having power on its own. History is full of examples of people who had power but failed to use it to benefit others. Instead, they used the power in harmful ways, usually at the expense of others' freedoms and rights, and sometimes at the expense of others' lives.

In these cases, power works in opposition to leadership. Instead of helping others ensure their survival and growth, people utilized their power to coerce others and mobilize them for selfish goals. Let us consider Hitler, who had the power of a nation and army behind him. What did he do with it? Was his country or the world any better off because of his actions?

We all know the answers. Instead of helping others, he chose to feed his own hungers and rigid, obsessive convictions, throwing the world into turmoil for at least 10 years (Germany suffered for longer).[25] Power clearly does not always inspire true leadership and love.

Many people who exercised inspiring acts of leadership started from a position without power. The same applies to untold numbers of heroes who choose to exercise leadership daily without power – you may be able to think of examples in your own life.

In 2015, Afroz Shah was appalled by the state of Versova Beach in India. He decided, with the help of his neighbor Harbansh Mathur, to don a pair of gloves and clean the coast.[26] He was able to mobilize volunteers from all walks of life to join in the efforts. After three years, Versova Beach is almost completely free from rubbish and plastic litter.[27] In fact, because of these efforts, sea turtles were able to hatch there after a 20-year hiatus.[28] Shah did not have power beyond the ability to act with his own two hands. Eventually, his acts of leadership earned him the United Nations' "Champion of the Earth" award in 2016. His efforts to clean the waters of India continue.[29]

Power is not a necessary condition to exercise leadership, but it can be a very useful tool if used wisely and purposefully, and it often comes as a consequence of exercising successful leadership (generally in an informal capacity).

ACTION TIP:

Avoid equating power with leadership, either from your own perspective or when looking for leadership in others. If you have power, use it to help others, but don't be dissuaded from acting just because you do not hold a powerful position.

LEADERSHIP MANTRA

I don't need to have power to do the right thing.
Doing the right thing is powerful enough.

LEADERSHIP IS NOT CONCERNED WITH LEAVING BEHIND A LEGACY

It is important that we do not think of leadership as a way to make our mark on the world from a selfish, egotistical point of view. Remember that the primary driving force must be about adding beneficial value, even if it involves not getting credit for doing so. Great acts of leadership usually do leave a legacy, but it is not the primary aim of those acts; it is not the true focus.

Legacy, or being remembered, is an ego-related issue, focused mainly on the "leader" and his/her actions. Remember, true leadership is not about the ones exercising it – it is not about us – but about others and adding value to their lives. Leadership is not about glory, glamour, fame, etc. Although there is nothing wrong with any of these concepts – they are often well-deserved by-products of exercising great leadership – they must not be the primary aim of leadership.

The person exercising leadership must not be seeking recognition as a "savior" or "hero." They act because they have spotted an opportunity to improve life for others, and they want to help others realize it. Exercising leadership is about waking THEM up to the possibilities of a better reality, and inspiring THEM to summon their courage and think creatively, so that THEY can make the leap forward out of misery, towards fulfillment.

When we decide to exercise leadership, we must ensure that our acts are not driven by selfish intentions. If we find ourselves asking, "how can I achieve fame and glory?" or "how can I leave behind a legacy?" then we may need to reconsider introducing change. If we have selfish motives, we cannot guarantee that our interventions are truly for the sake of others; we may cause instability and harm to satisfy our own egos. People exercising true leadership avoid exploiting the lives of others solely to leave behind a legacy or gain admiration.

For instance, Lyndon Johnson, who was the president that introduced many beneficial initiatives under "The Great Society" program, was also the president under whom the Vietnam War intensified. It was a war Johnson had inherited from his predecessor, John F. Kennedy, when Johnson became the 36th President of the United States after Kennedy's assassination. Johnson's drive to leave behind a positive legacy and his fear that losing face would tarnish his name and the efforts of "The Great Society" led him to prolong US involvement in a war that eventually stained his reputation and outlived his presidency.[30]

Unfortunately, given the confusing clutter surrounding this topic, some people have come to associate leadership predominantly with the attention or "spotlight" that often accompanies famous acts of leadership. They focus on the grandiosity that could be derived from the attention, and they don't see how that attention and importance may disappear if the act of leadership does not offer beneficial value. They lose sight of what leadership is truly about, and get caught up in amassing attention and power. Consequently, they introduce an initiative in the hopes of being remembered, without realizing that trying to leave a legacy behind is self-serving and has nothing to do with leadership.

Problems arise when glory-seeking "leaders" encounter the messy and dangerous aspects of leadership. If they are more committed to their own fame than to their cause, they may abandon it at the first sign of resistance, leaving the system shaken, or they may keep trying to force the initiative to work for fear of being seen as a failure. Either way, they will be unable or unwilling to deal with the messy and dangerous obstacles along the way.

Furthermore, an act driven by self-interests may serve no beneficial purpose, and will therefore automatically be excluded from the leadership discipline.

Leadership is not exercised as a means to achieve metaphorical immortality.

ACTION TIP:

Whenever you think about exercising leadership, you need to make sure that the driving force is not self-interest and glory, but that you intend to help people change and get unstuck. Be honest with yourself about your focus, and check in throughout the initiative to ensure it has not shifted.

If helping others is really your purpose for exercising leadership, success will also be your reward – you will see the people you care about flourish, and that may prove legacy enough for you.

LEADERSHIP MANTRA

My focus is on helping others create a better reality for themselves.

LEADERSHIP IS NOT NECESSARILY ABOUT REWARDS OR PUNISHMENTS

Rewards and punishments, in the conventional sense, are reserved for the discipline of authority. Authority uses them to influence the behavior of those who fall under their jurisdiction. An authority may exercise this power through the law (as a government official), through promotions and demotions (as an organizational executive), or through chores and allowances (as a parent or guardian).

People exercising leadership often don't have the authority to mete out conventional rewards and punishments. However, the tool can still be utilized in an unconventional sense. Rewards and punishments can come in psychological and emotional forms, such as encouragement, the prospect of loss, the fear of a negative future, and the hopes of a better reality. In this sense, they are part of the technology of leadership, and the person exercising leadership can utilize this tool to mobilize others.

It is important to understand that reward is not used as a way to bribe a person into supporting an initiative. It should only be used to mobilize and encourage them to make the choice to transform. Similarly, punishment is not used as a way to threaten a person into embracing a new reality, but to highlight the consequences of either going against the purpose or remaining stuck. Rewards and punishments are meant to inspire beneficial change and mobilize towards purposeful transformation.

As with other tools in the technology of leadership, how rewards and punishments are used can differentiate between an act of manipulation and an act of leadership.

For instance, when a person paints a realistic vision of a beautiful world to inspire and mobilize people to transform their lives for the better, this person will have exercised leadership. However, when management punishes a person for complaining about abusive work conditions, the misuse of this tool (punishment) is an act of coercion, control, and manipulation – it is not leadership.

The use of rewards and punishments does not automatically count as an act of leadership, and leadership may introduce an initiative without rewarding or punishing others. Sometimes, living in an elevated reality and fulfilling one's potential is reward enough, and failing this is perhaps punishment enough.

ACTION TIP:

If you have authority over others, avoid using this to manipulate them into following your initiative, either in a positive or negative way. You should not coerce or force people, even implicitly.

Don't stray into emotional punishments either – you shouldn't blackmail people by ending a friendship if they don't support you. Use rewards and punishments cautiously when you exercise leadership, assessing situations and people to ensure you are empowering rather than manipulating them.

LEADERSHIP MANTRA

My focus is on helping others create a better reality for themselves.

LEADERSHIP IS NOT EMPOWERMENT

This is a tricky one, because empowerment is often associated with acts of leadership. However, it is important to differentiate between two different forms of empowerment:

1. Empowerment can be exercised by offering individuals, often employees, constituents, etc., certain powers that allow them to carry out specific tasks. For instance, we may bestow upon our employees the power to make decisions on our behalf. In this case, this form of empowerment falls outside the discipline of leadership and is associated with authority. When we decide to delegate certain decisions or tasks to others, we need to have the power to make those decisions or carry out those tasks ourselves – a capacity associated with authority.

2. Empowerment can also come in the form of self-empowerment, where we inspire individuals to utilize their strengths and improve their lives. In this case, empowerment does fall into the realm of leadership. We don't necessarily have any power to give to others, but we help them to unlock power within themselves, allowing them to mature and become more self-reliant – we inspire them to use their inner power.

Therefore, leadership is not about concrete, distinguishable empowerment – that is a job for authority. It is about inspiring others to realize that they already have the tools to create a better reality, so they can empower themselves. Through inspiration and other forms of positive interventions, we mobilize them to unlock their inner power and build the necessary capacities to welcome change and realize a fulfilling life.

ACTION TIP:

Learn as much about self-empowerment as you can, and then look for ways to pass your understanding on to others so they can also unlock their potential. You are not looking to transfer power from yourself to others, but to help them realize it within themselves. Identify key strengths and highlight them to the relevant person, showing how they could use them to grow. Build self-confidence in those around you, and help them seek new opportunities.

LEADERSHIP MANTRA

Being human is immensely powerful by itself. My role is to evoke people's innate transformational power.

EXERCISING LEADERSHIP IS NOT ABOUT BEING SELF-RELIANT

Leadership is not a solo heroic adventure. Of course, we must commit ourselves fully to our initiatives if we wish to make a difference, but mobilizing people can be so daunting and so challenging that we may also need assistance.

Given the difficulties associated with change, some people will be reluctant to help. As we mentioned earlier, we may find ourselves alone at times. However, this does not mean that we should rely on ourselves without attempting to garner any support – having others by our side will help us deal with the obstacles and messiness of leadership, and will give us valuable, varied perspectives on our initiatives.

As an example of how a person exercising leadership may take help from others, consider a family unit. If one parent is trying to mobilize their child to make changes, they may need to turn to the other parent for support, or even just advice about the best way to approach the endeavor. In a school, a teacher might take support from other teachers when dealing with a difficult part of the curriculum.

Think about this on a bigger scale. Imagine we are attempting to mobilize a significant number of people, many of whom will be strangers. We cannot undertake this alone. We need people with us, if not to help us directly, at least as allies, partners, and supporters to help fend off the resistance and overcome the challenges.

Most movements, social reforms, and historical changes happened because the person or group exercising leadership did not attempt it alone. They had people supporting them and their initiatives. The Thirteenth Amendment would not have become a reality if Lincoln hadn't had a team of supporters and great social pressure to give his initiative strength.[31]

Remember, the more controversial and disruptive our acts of leadership are, the more intensely people are likely to resist them. If we are dealing with fierce resistance, we will need more support and help from those who empathize with our initiatives.

"Be strong enough to stand alone, smart enough to know when you need help, and brave enough to ask for it."

– *Unknown*

ACTION TIP:

Although leadership may sometimes be a lonely enterprise, attempting to exercise it without asking for help is not admirable, especially if you know that success in your endeavor will elevate the lives of others. Remember that if you have managed to inspire others with your initiative, they are likely to fiercely support you, so make sure you utilize all the resources at your disposal, including outside help.

LEADERSHIP MANTRA

When I need help, I have the strength to ask for it.

LEADERSHIP IS NOT ABOUT LEADING FROM THE FRONT OR THE BACK

I have read about how leadership is primarily focused on leading from the "back", while others argue that the focus should be on leading from the "front." It does not matter whether we lead from the front, back, left, right, or center. These are simply technical issues that depend purely on the nature of the challenge, the context, and the circumstances.

There are times when we must inspire individuals and lead by example; in such cases, we will be leading by "pull" (from the front). At other times, we will need to take a seat in the background and motivate people to lead themselves; in such a case we are leading by "push" (from the back). There are other times still where we need to be in the middle of the action, trying to motivate people to lead themselves through the chaos into a better reality.

We should lead from the point which the situation demands. Leadership is not about where we are situated, but about coming up with the best intervention and mobilizing others. Sometimes, it may even be necessary for the person exercising leadership to sit on the sidelines, and give others a chance to lead.

ACTION TIP:

Assess where you need to exert your energies, but stay adaptive. If you were "pushing" others forward but find they are not responding as you hoped, try "pulling" by providing an example in your own life. Be flexible and switch your approach when necessary.

LEADERSHIP MANTRA

The tactical position I lead from is irrelevant. I will lead from wherever I need to.

LEADERSHIP DOES NOT NECESSARILY GENERATE APPRECIATION

We should not undertake leadership for the sake of thanks. Our opponents won't thank us, and even our supporters may begrudge our efforts at times – we are making them uncomfortable, despite our best intentions.

Remember, we are doing what we are doing because we wish to benefit the lives of the people in the system, including ourselves. Although our work may warrant a "thank you," we must make sure gratitude is not our driving force. Expecting thanks could throw us off course if we don't receive it, and may damage our commitment to our initiatives.

Of course, we are likely to see some signs that people are grateful for our work. We may not get direct thanks, but we might notice people increasing their commitment to our initiatives, offering us help, or trying to contribute, and these are all signs of gratitude. We should not seek these as our primary goal, but should allow them to encourage us when we see them.

It is important to note that as the person exercising leadership, we must show others appreciation when they help us, even if we rarely receive it ourselves. Expressing gratitude will show that we acknowledge the difficulty of change, and those changing may become less resistant, or even more supportive.

That being said, when you receive thanks and appreciation for a good intervention, or for positively touching people's lives, give yourself permission to enjoy it, because it will enrich your soul and recharge you with energy and commitment. More importantly, accept it because you deserve it.

> "Real integrity is doing the right thing, knowing that nobody's going to know whether you did it or not."
>
> *– Oprah Winfrey*

Reflection

Think of a great leader whose story inspires you, and try to think of instances when they have received thanks for their work. There are many examples of people who have, but you will often find that even the greatest leaders were not expressly shown gratitude. They would have dealt with resistance, aggression, and accusation, and although they may have gained appreciation late in life, or long after their death, most of them faced immense difficulties before they were praised or rewarded for their actions.

ACTION TIP:

If you thrive on appreciation, look for subtle hints of it rather than expecting direct thanks. You are likely to find indications that people appreciate your efforts, but prepare yourself for a lack of even these. Remember that you are not leading for the sake of being thanked.

LEADERSHIP MANTRA

I don't do good to be appreciated. I do good because it is the right thing to do.

LEADERSHIP DOES NOT MIX WITH NEGATIVITY

We cannot exercise leadership with the mindset of a victim, with a blame mentality, or with feelings of guilt, shame, helplessness, hopelessness, or self-pity. These negative emotions are strong personal drivers and could be used to motivate people by energizing them with feelings of anger or sadness, but this is manipulation rather than leadership.

Acts of leadership should not be fueled by negative emotions. Even in times of turmoil, conflict, and injustice, trying to change the situation for the better must come from a positive place, fueled by optimism, hope, courage, confidence, forgiveness, love, and compassion. Transforming negative emotions into positive ones so they can be constructive is essential to leadership.

When Nelson Mandela was released from prison after 27 years in captivity, he set out to meet with many of the people responsible for his imprisonment and the continuation of apartheid. During those meetings, he neither condemned them nor sought revenge. Instead he showed one of his most prominent qualities: forgiveness.

Although the victims of apartheid had justifiable anger, Mandela showed the nation that they should not allow past injustices to stand in the way of turning over a new leaf. He believed that South Africa should be a nation built on the founding principle of equality for all. His ability to forgive inspired the nation, and helped people to mobilize to end racial segregation, turn over a new leaf, and work together to build a great South Africa.[32]

> "We must strive to be moved by a generosity of spirit that will enable us to outgrow the hatred and conflicts of the past."
>
> *– Nelson Mandela*

ACTION TIP:

When you are feeling negative, step away from your initiative and take time to refocus yourself. Address the negativity instead of just ignoring it, or it may affect your life without you realizing it. Use the magnanimity of great leaders to inspire you if you must forgive others, and review your feelings regularly to make sure you are building on positive foundations, not negative energy.

Be very wary of any kind of negative emotions, because emotions are not static. They can easily develop with time and turn into bitterness and resentment, and could even lead to violence.

LEADERSHIP MANTRA

Self-pity is powerless. Leadership is transformational empowerment.

LEADERSHIP IS NOT NECESSARILY ABOUT TEAMWORK

Often the task of leadership is a challenging one, because mobilizing people to change is a difficult undertaking. We need people to work with us, so that we can cooperate and coordinate our efforts with them in the process of mobilization. Remember, we often cannot do this alone.

Working with others requires a high degree of cooperation. However, we cannot say that every teamwork effort is by default an act of leadership, and that every team is exercising leadership. Sometimes, teamwork goes towards fulfilling certain tasks that don't require purposeful change. For instance, a surgical team is a group of experts working together, each in their own roles, to fulfill a medical task (e.g. surgery). This doesn't necessarily require an act of leadership, but possibly some team management skills.

Teamwork is a great thing, and we often need a collaborative spirit when mobilizing, but it is not a necessary condition of leadership. Teamwork relates more to management; it mainly involves coordination, collaboration, and a clear division of responsibility. We can achieve these managerial duties without exercising leadership.

If the changes we are advocating for are successful, others may be inspired to assume managerial roles and responsibilities as part of the transformation, and may seek to maintain the changes we have instigated, but we do not necessarily need to manage teams to exercise leadership.

For example, Jacob A. Riis was a journalist and author in the late 1800s. His book, *How the Other Half Lives*, brought attention to the poor slums that were occupied by more than sixty percent of the population of New York City in the year 1900. New York was not alone in having such squalid living quarters, and Riis' book was able to inspire numerous programs that worked to combat the situation.[33]

His work also inspired many more books, which in turn encouraged people and public offices to take action and elevate the realities of those who were living in terrible conditions. Riis did not have a team working with him to help him inspire others, but he brought light to the truth and, through his work, he mobilized others to make a change.

Sometimes, a few or all members of our own teams will abandon us and we might find ourselves alone. If leadership was contingent on teamwork, losing members of our own teams would jeopardize our ability to exercise leadership. However, this is not the case. We can still usually find ways to continue with our leadership acts and fulfill our purpose.

In the end, leadership is not dependent on teamwork, but having a team can help boost our efforts and encourage people to collaborate with each other.

ACTION TIP:

Do not allow the success of your plan to hinge on others working with you. Accept and utilize any help you are offered, but ensure you are not dependent on a team of people for the fulfillment of your purpose.

LEADERSHIP MANTRA

It would be great to lead as a team, but if I have to, I will do it alone.

LEADERSHIP IS NOT SIMPLE

It is said that leadership is not complicated, but I disagree. Everything we have talked about in this book, particularly the unpredictability of the people being mobilized (as individuals and groups), shows just how complicated trying to lead and mobilize others can be.

People are resourceful, creative, and imaginative, so when they resist, they will do so forcefully and sometimes unexpectedly. The nuances and intricacies of human nature mean that it can be challenging to anticipate their reactions, and this alone generates complexity. Throughout our leadership journeys, we will experience ups and downs, generated by both the people involved and by the different situations we encounter.

Sometimes even the best plans fail to reach the intended results, bringing about unintended consequences. When we are mobilizing groups, sometimes some individuals will fall through the cracks. Sometimes people fail to catch up and are left behind.

Even with the best intentions and extensive efforts made, it is inevitable that there will be some damage, adding more complexity to the situation. In the world of the military, even the best plans may result in "collateral damage" or "friendly fire." This adds to the highly complex nature of leadership.

The context of mobilizing people, organizations, and countries has a huge number of variables that are impossible to totally account for, control, or predict.

Most, if not all, of the people we try to mobilize will be carrying baggage, and have issues, triggers, scars, etc. They won't just have dreams, but also nightmares, demons, and phobias. They may get enthusiastic but then change their minds. They may be manipulated by opposing forces, populists, and demagogues who know how to pluck the right chords.

We will be asked many questions, and we may not always have the answers for these. There will be moments when we need to adapt to sudden changes in circumstances, and this will depend on our intuition and our flexibility. These things further complicate leadership.

We can have a general plan about where we want to go and what we want to achieve, but we all recognize that life is complex, has few guarantees, and is full of variables.

Exercising leadership cannot be simple – if it were, there would be fewer books about it.

ACTION TIP:

Look for active ways you can manage confusion and minimize the stress associated with chaos.

- You might do this by setting clear, easily achievable goals to give yourself a sense of progress.
- You might do this by documenting the positions of everyone involved in the initiative, and keeping these updated if things change.
- You could consider planning for potential scenarios before they become a reality.

Even with these steps, make sure you stay flexible and anticipate changes you haven't planned for. Adaptability will be your close friend during your leadership journey.

LEADERSHIP MANTRA

I'm ready for complexity, and I can be flexible if things suddenly change. It is not going to be easy, but it is going to be worth it.

LEADERSHIP IS NOT ABOUT GRANDIOSITY, GREATNESS, OR DOING GREAT THINGS

There is little doubt that the "leaders" mentioned in this book did great things, but leadership is not bound to a scale. Leadership isn't determined by the impact of the "leader's" actions.

Sometimes, the right intervention is one that is low-profile, one that only a handful of people even recognize. Provided its purpose is to mobilize people to consider better options and to seek an elevated reality, any act can be an act of leadership. It might avert a destructive situation, replace a reactive behavior with a purposeful and responsive one, avoid making a bad situation worse, or have some other similar benefit.

An act of leadership may be as simple as asking the right question, changing a single person's life, deciding to stay silent, or actively and consciously choosing to do nothing. If these are intended to enhance the lives of others, they are all acts of leadership, whether they are recognized or not.

Sometimes a subtle change can snowball, gain momentum, and create a big impact. The act itself does not need to be great for there to be significant change. Think about how a small spark lights the fuse that sets off beautiful fireworks to ignite the skies.

At times, the greatness we attribute to "great leaders" is a culmination of small interventions that created a better life for the people who were being mobilized. Everyday acts of great leadership are being carried out quietly by people worldwide, by people like you, honorable reader, and by people you know. Humans exercise millions of acts of leadership within our own contexts, mobilizing people around us either at home, work, or in our communities to do the right thing and help improve our realities.

These daily acts of leadership, like individual drops of rain filling a lake, have kept humanity surviving for thousands of years, and have led to the improvement of the human condition. It is the accumulation of these acts that is creating the beauty we see around us in the world today. We may not hear about many of them, but they are there, making things better.

For example, think about Maggie Doyne, who founded the non-profit foundation Blink Now. She started out by helping one orphan get an education, and has since opened a home and school for homeless children. Although she has had enormous impact on the lives of many, few of us will have heard of her – yet, there is no doubt that her interventions reflect purposeful acts of leadership.[34]

The dramatic speeches which we often see in films, rousing and mobilizing thousands, do not really reflect what an act of leadership is about. It can be dramatic, but the drama is not the point. Getting people's attention, getting noticed, is not what leadership focuses on. What matters is the purpose of the act.

Greatness in terms of leadership is not about the size or magnitude of a person's interventions. It is about the quality, meaning, and purpose that drove their acts of leadership.

Grandiosity is dispensable to those wishing to exercise leadership.

ACTION TIP:

Don't compare between initiatives, or worry that what you are working on is only a small-scale solution to a big problem. Very few of us have the power to change entire nations, but even if your intervention only makes life better for a single person, it is leadership and it is important. Don't get distracted from your cause.

LEADERSHIP MANTRA

It's better to make a difference on a small scale than to make no difference. I will take any opportunity to improve life for others, and will remember that tiny actions often set off avalanches of change.

LEADERSHIP DOES NOT MEAN BEING POPULAR

Being popular is not a necessary condition for exercising leadership. Some interventions might be welcomed because they reflect the yearning of the constituency for a better reality, but many leadership initiatives are not welcomed at all, at least not at first.

Remember that the pain which comes with change is not popular. We are the instigators of change, and therefore we should expect to suffer some unpopularity. If we look back at some of the most famous leaders in history, we see applause and accolades, but examining the contemporaries of the leaders – who often rejected, ridiculed, and tried to subdue them – will show us that this was rarely the case at the time. Indeed, many of the most world-renowned leaders were actually disliked by some of their own people.

It is the person's dedication to their purpose and their determination to see it through which has allowed them to win history's approval. If, at the time, they had focused on being popular, they would have swiftly abandoned their initiatives. The praise is an aftermath of the great improvements they wrought, and is rarely seen except in retrospect.

When we are mobilizing people and inspiring them to change, we should not think about the popularity of our interventions, or even consider whether our proposals will be accepted by everyone. If we know that change is necessary, and that it will benefit the system's survival and growth, we should push forward and not be dissuaded.

ACTION TIP:

As you should not expect gratitude, do not expect popularity. Avoid falling into the trap of going along with what is popular rather than what is right. Popularity often aligns with the ego, so focus on humility and use your sense of purpose and meaning to keep yourself traveling in the right direction. Remember also that popularity is a fair-weather friend, and will often come and go. Do not use it as an indicator of what is right for the system.

LEADERSHIP MANTRA

I'm driven by what I believe is right, regardless of whether it's popular or not.

LEADERSHIP DOES NOT ALWAYS ACHIEVE SUCCESSFUL RESULTS

Leadership aims to create a positive impact that will improve reality and bring about purposeful change. Unfortunately, there are times when something unexpected happens, and the act of leadership does not achieve the desired effect. Reality is complex and not always controllable. However, a failure does not necessarily mean that our capacity to lead is flawed, or that our interventions don't constitute acts of leadership.

On the contrary, even an intervention that doesn't bring about the desired change can still be considered a brilliant act of leadership. There are times when we will do everything right, but because of some uncontrollable factors, we won't get the intended results.

During the suffrage movement in the UK, women introduced multiple campaigns to pressure the parliament into granting them their voting rights. One movement, the suffragists, resorted to peaceful methods, favoring petitions and raising awareness through literature. Another movement, the suffragettes (born almost 8 years later), was founded by Emmeline Pankhurst and others. They introduced the "Deeds not Words" campaign, which resorted to more active and militant forms of protest (e.g. breaking windows using stones with messages attached, or attempting to storm the parliament). Despite the marches, petitions, sit-ins, hunger strikes, and other active and peaceful methods, it took almost 60 years and two laws (10 years apart) before women above the age of 21 could vote.[35]

Despite the time it took for the suffrage movement to reach its goal, many of the efforts of the movement throughout that time are still considered leadership.

Currently, there are many admirable efforts to introduce laws and policies to protect the environment. Many of these attempts have not succeeded to achieve their purpose. Are these not considered acts of leadership? Of course, they are. However, when the challenge is huge, it takes multiple attempts and initiatives to achieve the desired results and fulfill the purpose.

When we try to initiate purposeful change and the change fails, this does not mean that we have failed to exercise leadership, because this "wave of failure" may have laid the foundation for future attempts to follow and succeed.

Leadership is about introducing the right intervention without being discouraged by a suboptimal result. We need to be able to live with an unsatisfactory outcome, adapt, and keep trying. Even when our leadership initiatives yield no results, they are still leadership, provided they serve a clear and beneficial purpose.

Think about the founders of the major world religions. Some of the main principles that these religions teach are "peace," "love," "compassion," and "respect for others," but these religions have still been frequently misused to start conflict and war, corruption, and death. The negative results do not outweigh the intention behind the religious teachings, and the founders are not to blame for the actions of others. Their teachings were still acts of leadership, seeking to elevate and improve the lives of people around them.

If our leadership initiatives are doing more harm than good, then we need to consider whether to continue pursuing them. We may either need to temporarily put the initiatives on hold – and see if we can find a better way to introduce them at a later time – or we may need to call them off indefinitely – if we are unable to lead the initiatives and bring about positive change. However, this outcome does not imply that we were not exercising leadership.

Leadership specializes in navigating new and difficult terrain, and it can be hard to predict what the end result will be. Regardless of the result, if our acts have a beneficial purpose and mobilize others, they still count as acts of leadership. Remember, a failed leadership initiative can lay the groundwork for a successful one.

ACTION TIP:

Do not be discouraged if your initiative doesn't achieve the desired result. You will have made some positive changes, so pick yourself up and try again. Refuse to measure your ability to lead by the success or failure of a single initiative.

LEADERSHIP MANTRA

If an initiative doesn't achieve what I hoped it would achieve, it doesn't mean I have failed to lead.

LEADERSHIP IS NOT ABOUT SELF-SERVING AMBITIONS

I usually ask people who say their ambition is to become a "leader," president, or CEO: why? Some answers that I get reflect an underlying desire to gain power, status, fame, or wealth.

Ambition is often about a strong personal desire to fulfill a psychological need (e.g. attention, sense of accomplishment, sense of safety). Ambition can sometimes also be a disguise for greed, dominance, or hunger for power.

In this case, ambitions have little to do with leadership. Leadership is not about fulfilling self-centered ambitions, or realizing dreams to fulfill a self-serving vision.

Instead, ambitions are related to leadership when they are focused on service. It is tied to a desire to help others and elevate their lives, or to realize a vision that creates a beneficial reality for others and the system. It can be argued that the inspirations for leadership acts often stem from a desire to serve others.

For example, consider Abdul Sattar Edhi, dubbed by many as "Father Teresa." He set up the "Edhi Foundation," which has been operating for over 60 years. The foundation houses a large fleet of ambulances (1,500), which come to the aid of individuals around Pakistan. He has set up free orphanages, clinics, kitchens, nursing homes and more.[36] What inspired his acts of leadership?

It could be argued that he was motivated by his ambition. However, the differentiating factor is that his ambition comes from a place of service, and he shares this with his donors and volunteers.

Of course, there is nothing wrong with personal growth, with creating abundance for oneself, and with fulfilling personal dreams, if they are honorable and don't conflict with moral and ethical values. However, in the context of leadership, the emphasis is always on creating a better reality for others. Therefore, success and achievement are determined by whether the people, organization, or community has improved its conditions, and whether abundance has been created for all. The fruits of leadership are primarily for others to enjoy, ourselves included. The purpose is not self-serving.

"Leadership is a privilege to better the lives of others. It is not an opportunity to satisfy personal greed."

– *Mwai Kibaki*

ACTION TIP:

Make sure you are honest with yourself about your ambitions, and be aware of how they may influence your decisions. If you thirst for recognition, make sure this is not interfering with the initiative. Understanding your ambitions will allow you to keep them in check and ensure the focus of the initiative does not become self-serving.

LEADERSHIP MANTRA

Leading is about helping others fulfill their ambitions for a better life.

LEADERSHIP MUST NOT CREATE DEPENDENCY

The journey of leadership is often filled with obstacles; many people may turn to the person exercising leadership when they face trouble. This will inevitably create a sense of dependency. Although we may wish to help, we should be wary of fostering environments based on dependency. True leadership is about helping people build their capacities so that they can deal with their own journeys. We will not always be around, and there may be moments when we cannot offer assistance.

It may seem that this idea of leadership is harsh, but the reality is that if the person exercising leadership becomes the go-to person whenever there is trouble, people will not learn to deal with their own issues. Leadership is about building people's capacities to lead themselves, and fostering a dependent relationship will not do that.

For instance, during the Great Depression, former president of the United States, Franklin D. Roosevelt (FDR) introduced a series of programs collectively known as the "New Deal." Most of these programs targeted the unemployed, establishing new jobs and allowing people to work again and make a living. Part of the "New Deal" included legislation aimed at helping banks reestablish themselves and become functional once more. Instead of creating dependency, FDR created an environment that breathed life back into a nation, allowing individuals and organizations to get back on their feet.[37]

Let us consider an opposing example. In one country, people asked the senior government official representing their constituency to use his power and influence to get the government to build more schools in their neighborhoods. He replied to them that there was no need to trouble themselves with educating their children. After all, he was sending his son to the best schools so that he could get a top-notch education on their behalf. His son's education would increase his chances of replacing his father at a later time, and he would continue to care for the constituency and watch out for their "well-being".[38]

Shocking? Well, unfortunately it's a true story.

Of course, what he was actually doing was making sure that his constituency remained uneducated so that they would continue to rely on his family representing them in government. He was deliberately creating dependency to maintain his position of power, afraid that improving education levels might produce a number of other individuals who could contest him and run for public office.

ACTION TIP:

If you sense people are becoming dependent on you, look for ways to address this as quickly as possible. You may need to work to boost their self-confidence, perhaps by giving them achievable tasks which will empower them. Encourage others to take responsibility for their own journeys, and give them concrete evidence that they are competent enough to manage alone.

LEADERSHIP MANTRA

I know I have succeeded when I see people lead themselves towards progress.

CONCLUSION

Living is hard.

So, where do we go from here?

The truth is we are all able to exercise leadership. It is an intervention that any one of us can make whenever the opportunity presents itself. We may find ourselves in a situation where we can mobilize others (individuals or groups), whether at home, work, in the community, or out with friends, to elevate their consciousness and thinking, and help them create a better reality for themselves and the people around them.

I am sure that most people, including yourself, honorable reader, have exercised some form of leadership in their lives. If you really think about it, can you come up with a moment when someone said, "thank you for making me see things in a better way"? Take a few seconds to give yourself credit. You should be proud of yourself for making a difference and creating value in another person's life.

Our duty to exercise leadership is more pressing now than ever. At this time, we must exercise leadership in our own environments, wherever we are and whenever we can. The challenges that this world is destined to face in the 21st century are unprecedented. We have talked about the obstacles and opportunities that AI will pose, and the environmental crisis we may find ourselves facing. Exercising leadership is no longer a matter of luxury. It is time for us to have greater hope for the future of the world which we, and the people we care about, will live in.

For the foreseeable future, Earth is the only planet that we have to live on in this vast universe. If we don't each do our part, we are threatening the only home that we, our children, and the generations to follow, may ever know.

We must make changes and know that in the future, these changes will bear fruit. We might not get a chance to taste its sweetness or bitterness, but future generations, possibly even our children, will. It is up to us to hand over a world which is at least not worse off than the world we were left with. If we act now, exercising leadership, we increase our chances of handing them a world better than the one we inherited.

In many ways, we are living in the best times in known history. Our life expectancy and our medical knowledge are increasing, child mortality rates and poverty rates are falling, major diseases are being eradicated, violence is declining, and access to basics such as electricity is improving.

All of these achievements are consequences of the leadership acts of millions of people, and they are only scratching the surface of our progress. This gives us hope, and is proof of the impact and necessity of exercising value-driven, meaningful, and purposeful leadership.

Our survival and growth, and that of whom we love, are in our hands, largely dependent on our behavior, values, and mindsets. What we do and what we prioritize will determine whether we survive and grow.

Remember that leadership is about mobilizing others so that they can protect, celebrate, and cherish everything good that we say and do. At the same time, it is about mobilizing others to let go of everything bad, and to acquire the thinking and behavior that will help us all live better lives in less pain and more peace and joy.

For this to happen, we need to rethink our understanding of leadership and remove all the clutter that has surrounded this important notion. In addition to this, we need to take leadership back to its core and reattach a moral dimension to it. This dimension includes values like courage, sacrifice, truth, responsibility, love, authenticity, meaning, fulfillment, and other values that will help us live together on this celestial speck of stardust floating in the universe.

It is possible for all of us to live together with honor, dignity, peace, joy, generosity, inclusiveness, wealth, and prosperity. This is the challenge of leadership, and this is our invitation to act. It's our duty.

Life is hard.

We can make it bearable, and maybe beautiful, but certainly meaningful and worthwhile.

Lead whenever you can, because you do matter far more than you think.

Start with yourself.

Learn. Live. Lead.

NOTES

Why This Book

1. Schwab, Klaus. "The Fourth Industrial Revolution: What It Means and How to Respond." *World Economic Forum*, 14 Jan. 2016, www.weforum.org/agenda/2016/01/the-fourth-industrial-revolution-what-it-means-and-how-to-respond/.

2. "Benefits & Risks of Artificial Intelligence." *Future of Life Institute*, futureoflife.org/background/benefits-risks-of-artificial-intelligence/?cn-reloaded=1.

3. Hawksworth, J., Berriman, R., & Goel, S. "Will robots steal our jobs? An international analysis of the potential long term impact of automation". *PricewaterhouseCoopers*, 2018.

4. IPCC, 2018: Summary for Policymakers. In: *Global Warming of 1.5°C. An IPCC Special Report on the impacts of global warming of 1.5°C above pre-industrial levels and related global greenhouse gas emission pathways, in the context of strengthening the global response to the threat of climate change, sustainable development, and efforts to eradicate poverty* [Masson-Delmotte, V., P. Zhai, H.-O. Pörtner, D. Roberts, J. Skea, P.R. Shukla, A. Pirani, W. Moufouma-Okia, C. Péan, R. Pidcock, S. Connors, J.B.R. Matthews, Y. Chen, X. Zhou, M.I. Gomis, E. Lonnoy, T. Maycock, M. Tignor, and T. Waterfield (eds.)]. *World Meteorological Organization*, Geneva, Switzerland, pp. 32.

5. "Only 11 Years Left to Prevent Irreversible Damage from Climate Change, Speakers Warn during General Assembly High-Level Meeting | Meetings Coverage and Press Releases". *UN*, 28 Mar. 2019, March 28, https://www.un.org/press/en/2019/ga12131.doc.htm.

Putting Leadership in Perspective

1. Yuval Noah Harari. *Sapiens: A Brief History of Humankind*. Harper Perennial, 2018.

2. Ronald Heifetz, Alexander Grashow, and Martin Linsky. "The Theory Behind the Practice." *The Practice of Adaptive Leadership: TOOLS AND TACTICS for Changing Your Organization and the World*, Harvard Business Press, 2009, pp. 24

3. Ibid, pp. 28

4. Radford, Tim. "Evolution and Darwin." *The Guardian*, Guardian News and Media, 26 Apr. 2008, www.theguardian.com/science/2008/apr/27/genetics.darwinbicentenary.

Key Components of Leadership

1. "Mobilization (n.)." *Online Etymology Dictionary*, https://www.etymonline.com/word/mobilization.

2. "The Marathon of Hope - Terry Fox." *The Terry Fox Foundation*, https://terryfox.org/terrys-story/marathon-of-hope/.

3. "Terry's Story." *The Terry Fox Foundation*, https://terryfox.org/terrys-story/.

4. Hernandez, Vladimir. "Jose Mujica: The World's 'Poorest' President." *BBC News*, BBC, 15 Nov. 2012, https://www.bbc.com/news/magazine-20243493.

5. "Rosa Parks." *Biography.com*, A&E Networks Television, 29 Aug. 2019, https://www.biography.com/activist/rosa-parks.

6. "The Day Gandhi Began His Last Fast." *The Wire*, 13 Jan. 2018, https://thewire.in/communalism/the-day-gandhi-began-his-last-fast.

7. Amy McKenna. "Nelson Mandela." *The 100 Most Influential World Leaders of All the Time*. Britannica Educational Pub., 2010, pp. 295-297.

What Leadership Is

1. Doris Kearns Goodwin. "Transformational Leadership: Abraham Lincoln and the Emancipation Proclamation." *Leadership in Turbulent Times*, Simon & Schuster, 2018, pp. 211–242.

2. "Charles Manson." *Biography.com*, A&E Networks Television, 4 Dec. 2019, https://www.biography.com/crime-figure/charles-manson.

3. Rafferty, John P. "9 Infamous Assassins and the World Leaders They Dispatched." *Encyclopædia Britannica*, Encyclopædia Britannica, Inc., www.britannica.com/list/9-infamous-assassins-and-the-world-leaders-they-dispatched.

4. Young, Gayle. "Rabin's Assassination Has Parallels with Sadat's." *CNN*, Cable News Network, 6 Nov. 1995, edition.cnn.com/WORLD/9511/rabin/11-06/index.html.

5. Switzer, Kathrine. "The Girl Who Started It All." *Runner's World*, 26 Mar. 2007, https://www.runnersworld.com/runners-stories/a20801860/kathrine-switzer-runs-the-boston-marathon/.

6. Ibid.

7. Gombossy, George. "WHOLE FOODS SHOWS YOU CAN GET SOMETHING FOR NOTHING." *Courant.com*, 21 Dec. 2007, https://www.courant.com/news/connecticut/hc-xpm-2007-12-21-0712200494-story.html.

8. "Mother Teresa – Biographical". *NobelPrize.org*. https://www.nobelprize.org/prizes/peace/1979/teresa/biographical.; Pat Williams and Jim Denney. "Mother Teresa: In Service to God's Holy Poor." *21 Great Leaders Learn Their Lessons, Improve Your Influence*. Barbour Publishing, Inc., 2015, pp. 209-218.

9. Musk, Elon. "All Our Patent Are Belong To You." *Tesla, Inc.*, 12 June 2014, www.tesla.com/blog/all-our-patent-are-belong-you.

10. Alan Axelrod. "Dorothea Dix (1802-1887)." *The Disruptors: 50 People Who Changed the World*. Sterling, 2018, pp. 202-207.

11. Thunberg, Greta. "I'm Striking from School to Protest Inaction on Climate Change – You Should Too | Greta Thunberg." *The Guardian*, Guardian News and Media, 26 Nov. 2018, https://www.theguardian.com/ commentisfree/2018/nov/26/im-striking-from-school-for-climate-change-too-save-the-world-australians-students-should-too.; Alter, Charlotte, et al. "Greta Thunberg: TIME's Person of the Year 2019." *Time*, Time, 23 Dec. 2019, https://time.com/person-of-the-year-2019-greta-thunberg/.

12. Viktor E Frankl. *Man's Search for Meaning*. Rider, 2008.

13. Pooley, Eric. "Person of the Year 2001: Mayor of the World." *Time*, Time Inc., 31 Dec. 2001, content.time.com/time/specials/packages/ article/0,28804,2020227_2020306,00.html.; Powell, Michael. "In 9/11 Chaos, Giuliani Forged a Lasting Image." *The New York Times*, The New York Times, 21 Sept. 2007, www.nytimes.com/2007/09/21/us/politics/21giuliani.html.

14. "Top 10 Greatest Speeches - Susan B. Anthony." *Time*, Time Inc., 17 Sept. 2008, http://content.time.com/time/specials/packages/ article/0,28804,1841228_1841749_1841738,00.html.

15. "Susan B. Anthony's Speech on 'Woman's Right to The Suffrage' - 1873." *National Center*, https://nationalcenter.org/AnthonySuffrage.html.

16. *The Gettysburg Address*. Cornell University, https://rmc.library.cornell.edu/ gettysburg/good_cause/transcript.htm.

17. "Top 10 Greatest Speeches – Martin Luther King, Jr." *Time*, Time Inc., 17 Sept. 2008, http://content.time.com/time/specials/packages/ article/0,28804,1841228_1841749_1841741,00.html.

18. Max Tegmark. *Life 3.0: Being Human in the Age of Artificial Intelligence*. Vintage Books, 2018.

19. History.com Editors. "New Deal." *History.com*, A&E Television Networks, 29 Oct. 2009, https://www.history.com/topics/great-depression/new-deal.

20. Reilly, Lucas. "The Most Important Scientist You've Never Heard Of." *Mental Floss*, 17 May 2017, https://www.mentalfloss.com/article/94569/clair-patterson-scientist-who-determined-age-earth-and-then-saved-it.

21. Carlin, John. "Nelson Mandela: the Freedom Fighter Who Embraced His Enemies." *The Guardian*, Guardian News and Media, 7 Dec. 2013, https://www.theguardian.com/world/2013/dec/07/nelson-mandela-freedom-fighter-john-carlin.

22. Amy McKenna. "Martin Luther." *The 100 Most Influential World Leaders of All the Time*. Britannica Educational Pub., 2010, pp. 81-83.

23. A personal correspondence with Nelson Mandela in American University of Sharjah, Sharjah, United Arab Emirates on May 26th 2001.

24. Alan Axelrod. "Branch Rickey (1881 -1965)." *The Disruptors: 50 People Who Changed the World*. Sterling, 2018, pp. 238-242.

What Leadership Is Not

1. Based on a google search of the "synonyms of leadership"

2. Ronald Heifetz, Alexander Grashow, and Martin Linsky. "The Theory Behind the Practice." *The Practice of Adaptive Leadership: TOOLS AND TACTICS for Changing Your Organization and the World*, Harvard Business Press, 2009, pp. 24.

3. "Malala Yousafzai – Biographical". *NobelPrize.org*. https://www.nobelprize.org/prizes/peace/2014/yousafzai/biographical

4. "Encyclopedia of Business 2nd Ed. - Management." *Reference for Business*, https://www.referenceforbusiness.com/encyclopedia/Kor-Man/Management.html.

5. Griffith, Erin. "Startups Are Failing Because They Make Products No One Wants." *Fortune*, Fortune, 2 Mar. 2015, fortune.com/2014/09/25/why-startups-fail-according-to-their-founders/.; Neiditch, Daniel. "All Entrepreneurs Face Failure But the Successful Ones Didn't Quit." *Entrepreneur*, 15 Jan. 2018, www.entrepreneur.com/article/306867.

6. "Margaret Thatcher, Prime Minister" in: Walsh, Bryan. "The Great Introverts and Extroverts of Our Time." *Time*, Time, 26 Jan. 2012, http://healthland.time.com/2012/01/27/the-great-introverts-and-extroverts-of-our-time/slide/margaret-thatcher-prime-minister/.

7. "Mohandas Gandhi, Revolutionary" in: Walsh, Bryan. "The Great Introverts and Extroverts of Our Time." *Time*, Time, 26 Jan. 2012, http://healthland. time.com/2012/01/27/the-great-introverts-and-extroverts-of-our-time/slide/ mohandas-gandhi-revolutionary/.

8. Perry, Mark. "When Presidents Get Angry." *POLITICO Magazine*, 27 Sept. 2017, https://www.politico.com/magazine/story/2017/09/27/donald-trump-anger-215648.

9. Black, Christina. "A U.S. Presidential Leadership Lesson: Optimism." *UVA Today*, University of Virginia, 20 Feb. 2017, https://news.virginia.edu/ content/us-presidential-leadership-lesson-optimism.

10. Shenk, Joshua Wolf. "Lincoln's Great Depression." *The Atlantic*, Atlantic Media Company, 1 Oct. 2005, https://www.theatlantic.com/magazine/ archive/2005/10/lincolns-great-depression/304247/.; Doris Kearns Goodwin. "Transformational Leadership: Abraham Lincoln and the Emancipation Proclamation." *Leadership in Turbulent Times*, Simon & Schuster, 2018, pp. 211–242.

11. Addison, Dr. Paul. "History - World Wars: Why Churchill Lost in 1945." *BBC*, BBC, 17 Feb. 2011, http://www.bbc.co.uk/history/worldwars/wwtwo/ election_01.shtml.

12. Klein, Christopher. "Winston Churchill's World War Disaster." *History.com*, A&E Television Networks, 21 May 2014, https://www.history.com/news/ winston-churchills-world-war-disaster.

13. "Gallipoli Casualties by Country." *New Zealand History*, https://nzhistory. govt.nz/media/interactive/gallipoli-casualties-country.

14. Addison, Dr. Paul. "History - World Wars: Why Churchill Lost in 1945." *BBC*, BBC, 17 Feb. 2011, http://www.bbc.co.uk/history/worldwars/wwtwo/ election_01.shtml.

15. Lohnes, Kate. "The Jungle." *Encyclopædia Britannica*, Encyclopædia Britannica, Inc., 19 Dec. 2019, https://www.britannica.com/topic/The-Jungle-novel-by-Sinclair.; "BRIA 24 1 b Upton Sinclair's The Jungle: Muckraking the Meat-Packing Industry." *Constitutional Rights Foundation*, https://www.crf-usa.org/bill-of-rights-in-action/bria-24-1-b-upton-sinclairs-the-jungle-muckraking-the-meat-packing-industry.html.

16. Pat Williams and Jim Denney. "Gandhi: The Great Soul." *21 Great Leaders: Learn Their Lessons, Improve Your Influence*. Barbour Publishing, Inc., 2015, pp. 199-208.; Alan Axelrod. "Mohandas Gandhi (1869 -1948)." *The Disruptors: 50 People Who Changed the World*. Sterling, 2018, pp. 219-225.

17. "Mission." *4Ocean*, 4Ocean, https://4ocean.com/mission/.

18. The Editors of Encyclopaedia Britannica. "Jim Jones." *Encyclopædia Britannica*, Encyclopædia Britannica, Inc., 14 Nov. 2019, https://www.britannica.com/biography/Jim-Jones.

19. "Dogma." *Lexico Dictionaries | English*, Lexico Dictionaries, https://www.lexico.com/en/definition/dogma.

20. A personal experience with country officials of the Sultanate of Oman in 2019 regarding Oman's 2040 vision.

21. History.com Editors. "Adolf Hitler." *History.com*, A&E Television Networks, 29 Oct. 2009, https://www.history.com/topics/world-war-ii/adolf-hitler-1.

22. Pat Williams and Jim Denney. "Gandhi: The Great Soul." *21 Great Leaders Learn Their Lessons, Improve Your Influence*. Barbour Publishing, Inc., 2015, pp. 199-208.; Alan Axelrod. "Mohandas Gandhi (1869 -1948)." *The Disruptors: 50 People Who Changed the World*. Sterling, 2018, pp.218-225.

23. Alan Axelrod. "Frederick Winslow Taylor (1856-1915)." *The Disruptors: 50 People Who Changed the World*. Sterling, 2018, pp. 105-109.

24. "Lives on the Line: The High Human Cost of Chicken." *Oxfam America*, 23 May 2018, https://www.oxfamamerica.org/livesontheline/.

25. History.com Editors. "Adolf Hitler." *History.com*, A&E Television Networks, 29 Oct. 2009, https://www.history.com/topics/world-war-ii/adolf-hitler-1.

26. UN Environment Programme. "Afroz Shah." *Champions of the Earth*, https://www.unenvironment.org/championsofearth/laureates/2016/afroz-shah.

27. Toner, Kathleen. "He's doing the dirty work to keep plastic out of the ocean." *CNN*, Cable News Network, 17 Oct. 2019, https://edition.cnn.com/2019/10/17/world/cnnheroes-afroz-shah-afroz-shah-foundation/index.html.

28. Safi, Michael. "Mumbai Beach Goes from Dump to Turtle Hatchery in Two Years." *The Guardian*, Guardian News and Media, 30 Mar. 2018, https://www.theguardian.com/world/2018/mar/30/mumbai-beach-goes-from-dump-to-turtle-hatchery-in-two-years.

29. Toner, Kathleen. "He's doing the dirty work to keep plastic out of the ocean." *CNN*, Cable News Network, 17 Oct. 2019, https://edition.cnn.com/2019/10/17/world/cnnheroes-afroz-shah-afroz-shah-foundation/index.html.

30. Doris Kearns Goodwin. "Visionary Leadership: Lyndon Johnson and Civil Rights." *Leadership in Turbulent Times*, Simon & Schuster, 2018, pp. 306–343.

31. Doris Kearns Goodwin. "Transformational Leadership: Abraham Lincoln and the Emancipation Proclamation." *Leadership in Turbulent Times*, Simon & Schuster, 2018, pp. 211–242.

32. Mutch, Barbara. "Mandela Taught the Power of Forgiveness: Column." *USA Today*, Gannett Satellite Information Network, 8 Dec. 2013, https://www.usatoday.com/story/opinion/2013/12/08/nelson-mandela-remember-column/3896245/.

33. Alan Axelrod. "Jacob A Riis (1849-1914)." *The Disruptors: 50 People Who Changed the World*. Sterling, 2018, pp. 214-218.

34. "Our History." *BlinkNow*, BlinkNow Foundation, https://blinknow.org/pages/our-history.

35. Myers, Rebecca. "General History of Women's Suffrage in Britain." *The Independent*, Independent Digital News and Media, 28 May 2013, www.independent.co.uk/news/uk/home-news/general-history-of-women-s-suffrage-in-britain-8631733.html.

36. Masood, Salman. "Abdul Sattar Edhi, Pakistan's 'Father Teresa,' Dies at 88." *The New York Times*, The New York Times, 9 July 2016, https://www.nytimes.com/2016/07/09/world/middleeast/abdul-sattar-edhi-pakistans-father-teresa-dies-at-88.html.

37. History.com Editors. "New Deal." *History.com*, A&E Television Networks, 29 Oct. 2009, https://www.history.com/topics/great-depression/new-deal.

38. A story heard in person about a late prominent Lebanese politician.

ABOUT THE AUTHOR

Michael Kouly began his career as a Reuters war journalist. He covered armed conflicts that involved, Israel, Lebanon, Syria, Iran, Hezbullah, Islamic extremists, terrorism, the United States, Kuwait, Iraq and others... He also covered musical concerts, fashion shows and car racing.

Writing about wars, geopolitics, international diplomacy, and global events offered Michael unique opportunities to witness, analyze and write about leadership at the highest levels: where bad leadership meant the loss of thousands of lives and good leadership led to avoiding wars, saving lives and rebuilding shattered countries.

Michael also exercised corporate leadership over a period of 30 years as he led the growth of regional and international businesses. He is a three-time CEO and president at organizations like Reuters, Orbit and Cambridge Institute for Global Leadership, managing people in more than 20 countries.

Over the span of his career, Michael made some good decisions that generated remarkable success and also some not so good decisions that

offered valuable lessons on what works and what doesn't when exercising leadership - emphasizing the mindset of "you either win or learn".

From as far back as he can remember, Michael has been fascinated by leadership. He has spent his life learning about leadership, purpose and strategy by practicing them, watching others lead and by conducting extensive research on the art and science of mobilizing people and organizations towards growth and noble purposes.

Michael is a World Bank Fellow, author and keynote speaker about leadership, strategy, purpose and international politics. He is the founder of the Kouly Institute and the creator of unique Executive Leadership Programs, that have been delivered to thousands of top business executives, NGO's and government leaders worldwide.

He also dedicates time to various non-profit organizations such as the Middle East Leadership Academy (MELA), Central Eurasia Leadership Academy (CELA), South East Asia Leadership Academy (SEALA) and Leaders Across Boarders (LAB).

His calling is to help people, organizations and countries lead purpose driven lives.

Michael studied at Harvard and Princeton Universities, and is an advisor to state leaders.

OTHER BOOKS BY THE AUTHOR

BOOK 1 OF THE
SELF-LEADERSHIP BOOK SERIES

FINDING YOUR HUMMUS

This book will provide you, your colleagues, family and friends with insights about life and business to unleash your personal and organizational power.

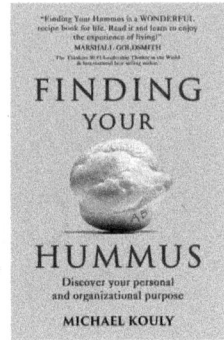

"Finding Your Hummus is a WONDERFUL recipe book for life. Read it and learn to enjoy the experience of living!"
MARSHALL GOLDSMITH
The Thinkers 50 #1 Leadership Thinker in the World & best-selling author

FINDING
YOUR

HUMMUS
Discover your personal
and organizational purpose

MICHAEL KOULY

- Shift happens in life and business, are you ready?

- What is the prime philosophy behind starting a business of growth and sustainable success?

- Do you, your people and business have a guiding purpose? This book is about finding your calling.

- Do you have a personal and organizational strategy to fulfill your purpose? This book is about self awareness, self motivation and self leadership that together can achieve self fulfillment.

- How do you deal with competition, conflict and confusion? This book is rich with empowering inspirational quotes that generate strength and lead to self actualization.

- What is the mindset to lead a life of resilience, abundance and significance? This book is about finding your passion and discovering your way of living a purpose driven life.

BOOK 2 OF THE
SELF-LEADERSHIP BOOK SERIES

If I didn't
Give A ....
I would...

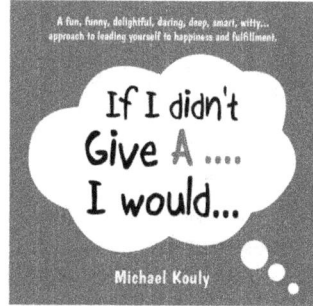

A fun, funny, delightful, daring, deep, smart, witty... approach to leading yourself to happiness and fulfillment.

If I didn't
Give A ....
I would...

Michael Kouly

As you will discover,this entertaining book of insightful and witty humor is not like other self leadership books.

WHILE ENJOYING THE EXPERIENCE OF THIS BOOK, YOU'LL ALSO:

- **Blow off steam:** We all have personal issues, challenges, and obstacles that accumulate stress that must be released to keep us in a state of peak motivation.

- **Know yourself:** Sometimes an entire life is spent being stuck at the expense of personal, business, social and relational opportunities for success. Self-discovery is the first step to the healing, actualization, and optimization of your life.

- **Reflect:** Recognizing your priorities, what you really want and what matters most to you is the key to your growth in all aspects of your life.

- **Decide:** To solve problems and catch opportunities, decisions are needed. This book will help you decide and act to expand your potential in a fun, playful, smart and effective way.

- **Lead:** True leadership starts with the self where smart and effective strategy, action and execution are the keys to the growth of our capacity.

BOOK 3 OF THE
SELF-LEADERSHIP BOOK SERIES

MUTE

It doesn't matter who you are or what you do. You carry voices in your head, voices that are always talking to you. Some of the voices whisper, others shout. Some make logical arguments, others create dramas.

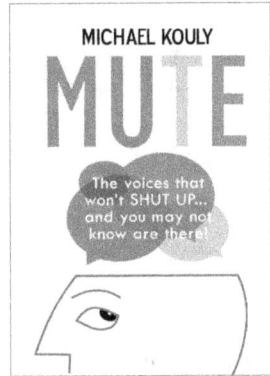

MICHAEL KOULY

MUTE

The voices that won't SHUT UP... and you may not know are there!

Do you know the voices in your head? Do you know where they've come from and how they are controlling you?

As soon as you meet a person, you begin to carry their voice with you. This starts with your parents, loved ones, hated ones, bosses, spouses, heroes, and everyone who is or was significant in your life.

What do these voices want? They want you to live life their way.

What about your freedom? Well, this book is about exactly that: exercising your freedom.

We will look at how you can willingly listen to the encouraging voices and mute the negative ones.

We want to give you the tools to live a happy, successful and fulfilling life that is aligned with your personal purpose and best self.

Life is a blink. There is no time to waste living under the influence of negative voices. Read this book, share it with others, and learn how to lead a life of freedom and meaning so you can become a beautiful voice in the heads of those around you.

BOOK 4 OF THE
SELF-LEADERSHIP BOOK SERIES

FORGET
HAPPINESS

MICHAEL KOULY

FORGET
HAPPINESS

Seven Steps to a Fulfilled Life

Read this book and fill your life with joy.

You deserve it.

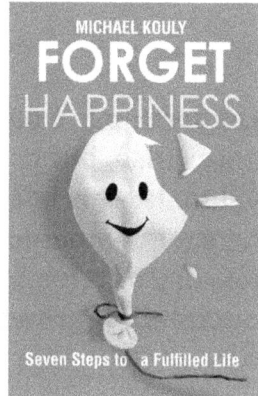

This unique book offers a practical, clear, and realistic roadmap for reaching fulfillment. It is a pleasant and easy read that will lift your spirits, encourage you, and help you discover and love your beautiful self so that you may live a life of purpose, meaning, beauty, and joy.

We live in the most comfortable and exciting time in history, and yet stress, anxiety, depression, suffering, and inner emptiness are greater than ever before, even among the rich and successful. Happiness has become a tired buzzword. An increasing number of self-help books idealize and promise it, yet it remains frustratingly elusive.

This book asks you to stop looking for happiness because happiness cannot be found on its own. Happiness is an outcome, a result, a consequence of living a life of fulfillment. When you align your life with your true self and feel fulfilled, deep happiness, joy, and inner peace will become part of your natural state.

WIDE OPEN

Leadership is a dangerous enterprise, but the rewards are valuable. This book is designed to be your companion in your thrilling journey of remarkable survival and outstanding growth.

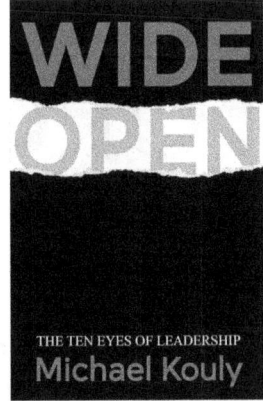

THE TEN EYES OF LEADERSHIP
Michael Kouly

THIS UNIQUE AND ILLUMINATING BOOK WILL OPEN YOUR EYES WIDE, SO YOU LEARN MORE ABOUT:

- **Authority:** You are surrounded by authority figures such as parents, bosses, CEOs, presidents, or governments. As you already know, not understanding how to deal with authority is risky.

- **Enemies:** Enemies are a fact of life. They could be passive or aggressive. Enemies want to undermine you and your acts of leadership. Not understanding how to deal with enemies is dangerous.

- **Understanding Yourself and Others:** It is hard to survive and grow and to lead yourself without understanding what drives your thoughts, feelings, words, actions, behaviors, dreams, and ambitions. It is impossible to lead others without understanding them first.

- **Understanding Systems:** We live and work in systems. A system can be a family, team, company, community, city, country or the world. Systems have their unique psychology and rules. Not understanding systems will put your existence and progress at risk, as you may be excluded or isolated from the group that you belong to.

HOW TO TRUMP THE ENEMY

HOW TO TRUMP THE ENEMY

Strategies for Trumping Your Leadership Opponents

MICHAEL KOULY

Some people love you and some don't. When you exercise leadership, some will support you and others will resist, oppose, obstruct, sabotage, or obsessively fight you until you lose.

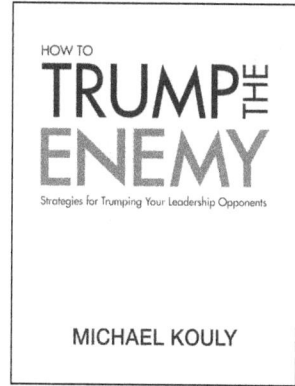

Most attempts at leadership fail not because of how allies are utilized, but because many leaders lack the vital skills necessary for dealing with adversaries.

What will determine your leadership success is mainly your ability to handle those who stand against you.

THIS BOOK IS A UNIQUE AND COMPREHENSIVE REFERENCE THAT YOU CAN CONSULT EVERY TIME YOU DEAL WITH RESISTERS, OPPONENTS, OR ENEMIES.

YOU WILL LEARN MORE ABOUT:

- **Strategies:** There are 104 strategies that you can use separately or in combinations as per the specific nature of the resistance that you are facing.

- **Scenarios:** There are 36 separate scenarios covering seven types of personal, social, organizational, business, and political opponents.

- **Intensities:** There are six intensities of opposition that start from passive and escalate to passive-aggressive, active, active-aggressive, malevolent, and finally archenemy.

- **You:** There is a chapter on YOU acting as your own enemy by allowing your dysfunctional mindsets, beliefs, and habits to sabotage your growth and prevent you from being all that you can be.

BEYOND
STRATEGY

WHY "BEYOND STRATEGY"?

Many people find strategy intimidating, complex, or abstract, but it doesn't have to be.

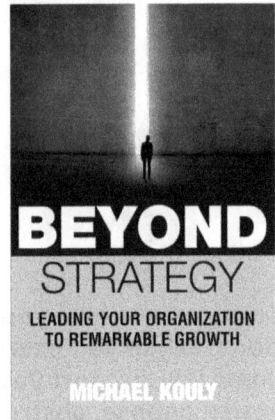

BEYOND
STRATEGY
LEADING YOUR ORGANIZATION
TO REMARKABLE GROWTH

MICHAEL KOULY

This book presents a new way of thinking about strategy that is uniquely based upon the Purpose-Driven Growth Model (PDG), in which your organization's purpose and profitability is key to guiding its growth.

- It explores strategy concisely and thoughtfully, examining what the concept encompasses and how strategies can be constructed in a fast-changing and uncertain world.

- It illustrates the differences between strategies that flourish and strategies that languish, and delves into the reasons driving each outcome.

- It offers comprehensive thinking, and tools which view strategy holistically, emphasizing how to lead organizations towards sustainable growth and exceptional performance.

The PDG Model sketches out a practical hybrid of strategy and leadership, that must be unified to fulfill organizational purpose, create growth, and deliver profits. Leadership without strategy is futile, and strategy without leadership is doomed. The two must synchronize to produce results.

www.ingramcontent.com/pod-product-compliance
Lightning Source LLC
Chambersburg PA
CBHW060420200326
41518CB00009B/1419